Sty/us

COPYRIGHT © 2010 BY STYLUS PUBLISHING, LLC.

Published by Stylus Publishing, LLC
22883 Quicksilver Drive
Sterling, Virginia 20166-2102

Library of Congress Cataloging-in-Publication Data
Building teaching capacities in higher education: a
comprehensive international model / edited by Alenoush
Saroyan and Mariane Frenay.
    p.   cm.
Includes index.
    ISBN 978-1-57922-410-3 (cloth : alk. paper)
    1. College teachers—Training of—Case studies.
2. Universities and colleges—Faculty—Case studies.
3. Education, Higher—Case studies.   4. Curriculum
enrichment—Case studies.   5. Academic achievement—
Case studies.   I. Saroyan, Alenoush, 1949-   II. Frenay,
Mariane, 1965.
LB1738.B76   2010
378.1'2—dc22   2009026911

13-digit ISBN: 978-1-57922-410-3 (cloth)

Printed in the United States of America

All first editions printed on acid free paper
that meets the American National Standards Institute
Z39-48 Standard.

Bulk Purchases

Quantity discounts are available for use in workshops
and for staff development.
Call 1-800-232-0223

First Edition, 2010

10   9   8   7   6   5   4   3   2   1

BUILDING TEACHING CAPACITIES IN HIGHER EDUCATION

A Comprehensive International Model

Edited by

Alenoush Saroyan

and *Mariane Frenay*

Prologue by James Groccia

STERLING, VIRGINIA

BUILDING TEACHING CAPACITIES
IN HIGHER EDUCATION

This book is dedicated to all those who, in one way or another, promote and support educational development, and work tirelessly and imaginatively to improve the quality of teaching and learning in universities worldwide.

CONTENTS

ACKNOWLEDGMENTS

We wish to acknowledge the support of The Human Resources and Skills Development of Canada and the European Commission and its Director General of Education and Culture for the EU/Canada Program for Cooperation in Higher Education and Vocational Education and Training that recognized our project as innovative and funded it. The FACDEV project was instrumental in forging strong links among a group of academics who are dispersed around the globe. Our collaboration continues to date, even after funding has long stopped. This book, one of many by-products of the project, is a good example of how one small project may bear unexpected results and give birth to a wealth of stimulating ideas. It also tells a story of mutual enrichment and is a model of how a community of practice that shares common values can be developed and sustained over time.

Context: The FACDEV Mobility Project

Alenoush Saroyan and Mariane Frenay

The story of this book is probably a common one in our field. It is the story of exchanging ideas, dreaming of a better educational world, and getting the chance to put some ideas into practice. The seed was planted with informal and bilateral conversations among colleagues. We arrived at the idea of engaging in a joint project and looking for funding opportunities that would provide a formal structure to support this collaboration. That opportunity came with the launching of the European branch of the UNESCO Global University Network on Innovation (GUNI) that took place at the Université catholique de Louvain, in Louvain-la-Neuve in February 2002. The meeting was an opportunity for Canadian and European colleagues to meet and exchange views on important research issues in higher education as well as practices of faculty development. Subsequently, we took advantage of the chance to apply for a Student Mobility Project, funded jointly by the European Commission and its Director General of Education and Culture and by The Human Resources and Skills Development of Canada. We received a grant for three years starting in 2002 for our "FACDEV" project to promote the practice of faculty development and develop a curriculum for training graduate students in this area.

As it turned out, the gains of the project were much greater than the deliverables specified in our contracts with our respective funding bodies. This project involved more than simply eight individuals from eight institutions and five different countries. It brought together eight teams, all involved in one way or another in faculty development research and practice. Working meetings took us to different universities on both sides of the Atlantic where we were able to experience and share the everyday life of other university cultures. Through constructive interactions, we forged strong professional and personal friendships that have continued beyond the life of the project and resulted in numerous collaborations. This book, one of many by-products of the project, is a good example of how one small project may bear unexpected results and give birth to a wealth of stimulating ideas. It also tells a story of mutual enrichment and is a model of how a community of practice that shares common values can be developed and sustained over time.

International Experience and Collaboration in Our Student Mobility Project

Faculty development as a field of practice in Europe and Canada is very diverse in both history and practice. In Canada, student discontent about the quality of education, voiced strongly through student demonstrations across North American campuses in the 1960s, promoted the creation of teaching and learning units in universities. It took a while before every institution could claim it was investing resources in teaching development, but today almost all 93 Canadian universities have some formal way of supporting faculty teaching and student learning. In Europe, this tradition is quite varied, ranging from full-fledged development (such as in the Scandinavian countries and the UK) to almost no faculty development activities (such as in France).

Our program, entitled FACDEV: Promoting Faculty Development to Enhance the Quality of Learning in Higher Education and funded jointly by the EU/Canada Program for Cooperation in Higher Education and Vocational Education and Training (2002–2005), was developed to fill the gap created by the absence of formal training programs in this area. More specifically, it sought to develop an international formal academic program in higher education, with specific focus on faculty development (Frenay et al., 2005). The target audiences for this program were doctoral students who wished to specialize in faculty development or to complement their graduate education with formal knowledge of university teaching and learning. As well, the program included faculty developers and university professors who wished to develop a more profound understanding of university pedagogy.

Because we wanted the project to be sustainable beyond the three-year funding period, we set out to develop a curriculum as a first step and to engage in a student exchange[1] process as a subsequent step. Thus, an important goal of the project was to prepare a common curriculum that would benefit graduate students participating in the project. For this curriculum,

we envisioned a common foundation, or core course, that all student participants, regardless of home institution, would take at the outset. In addition,
we proposed that each host institution provide one complementary course
option, based on existing expertise in that institution. We also envisioned a
practicum component for the program. Visiting students would engage in
two practica. In one, they would disseminate within the host institution a
particular expertise they had gained in their home institution. In the other,
visiting students would acquire a new skill or knowledge about an innovative
practice and process while at the host institution and, on their return, would
disseminate this newly gained insight within their home institution. Thus,
the students would become vehicles for exchanging ideas and practices and,
more important, would be able to practice an aspect of faculty development
in authentic contexts. Figure 1 illustrates the components of our proposed
program.

In addition to exchange of students, the project supported exchange of
faculty.[2] We anticipated that these visits would provide an opportunity to
contribute to the practice of faculty development internationally and to learn
about the scope and ways in which different programs are implemented in
different institutions and cultural contexts.

The concept we were promoting was clearly based on a distributed learning model. It was our vehicle to create and nurture a community of practice,
enriched and informed by a range of expertise and different higher education
traditions, cultures, and languages.

The Canadian partners of the project were McGill University (lead
Canadian institution), University of Manitoba,[3] and Université de Sherbrooke. The European partners were Université catholique de Louvain
(UCL) (lead EC institution) and its Flemish sister, Katholieke Universiteit
Leuven (KUL), both Belgian institutions; Aalborg University in Denmark;
and Université de Bourgogne in France. In addition, the Swiss Réseau
romand de Conseil, Formation et Evaluation pour l'enseignement universitaire contributed to this project as an associate partner by participating in
the program evaluation component.

This project was innovative on several counts. First, it sought to develop
and disseminate an international curriculum through a collaborative process
among multiple institutions with diverse cultural and higher education traditions. Second, it promoted university teaching and learning by conceptualizing faculty development as a formal academic discipline. Third, it offered a

FIGURE 1
FACDEV Program Components

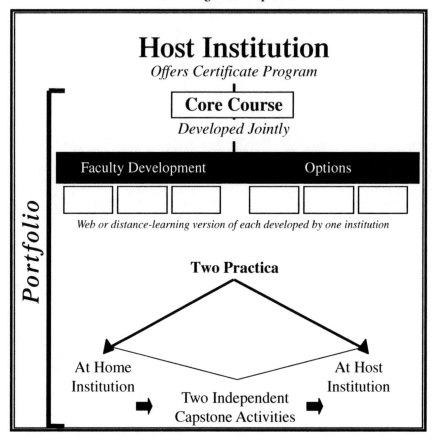

unique opportunity for students and staff to formally prepare and train for academic careers by developing solid grounding in university pedagogy. Finally, it was a resolute step toward preparing tomorrow's academics to become agents of change who could help improve the quality of teaching and learning.

For the European partners, the primary additional gain was exposure to a well-developed and more comprehensive practice of faculty development, different from existing European practices. For the Canadian partners, the occasion provided exposure to educational and professional approaches that did not have a North American perspective and the opportunity to connect with the wider European community of practitioners and researchers in the field, and it enabled them to benefit from the vision and aims of the Bologna process[4] and engage directly and indirectly in advancing some of its goals.

We undertook the Mobility Project with a strong practice orientation. We believed that by systematically observing, sharing, and analyzing our respective national perspectives on educational development practice, the practice in each country would benefit. In the shared experience of the project, we soon realized the synergy of Rowland's (1999) interaction in private (practice), public (theory), and shared (critical debate) contexts.

One of the fundamental gains for all project participants was consolidation of our understanding of what our field was about. We came to this through a process of what Bransford et al. (2006) refer to as "searching for a conceptual collision" (p. 229). Our different perspectives about faculty development helped us, first, to tease apart our "tacit assumptions" about our field and then to compare them. From this process evolved new understandings of the scope and meaning of faculty development to the extent that we felt what we envisioned was not just *faculty development* but rather *educational development*. In addition, we were able to identify tensions underlying the practice of educational development and consider challenges ahead for each country and for the field as a whole. When we undertook this Mobility Project, we did not anticipate that one of the significant outcomes of our collaboration would be a framework that conceptualizes a broadly shared practice and scholarship in educational development. The opportunity to generate this framework and to be able subsequently to expose it to other practitioners for criticism and input was a delightful unexpected bonus.

The Concept of the Book

Even though the genesis of the idea of this book was our FACDEV Mobility Project, this book is not about that project. It is about the meaning and practice of faculty and educational development, and how this field of practice and research may address challenges confronting higher education institutions worldwide. Just as we were able to develop a nucleus network of collaborative partners, we believe that the larger international network of educational developers can develop into a strong advocate for important higher-education policy with respect to building teaching and learning capacity in our universities.

The chapters have been written and edited with three objectives in mind. The first is to ground the concept of educational development in concrete examples of units or centers with an explicit mission to improve and promote the teaching and learning capacities of universities. The second is to demonstrate that faculty/educational development expertise exists and is developing. The third is to provide our colleagues around the world with a framework and model of educational development that can serve a number of purposes, including professional development, monitoring and assessment of effectiveness, and research.

Because of the comprehensive scope of this framework, we think the book would be of interest to different stakeholders. First and foremost, it is a solid reference for faculty/staff/educational developers and other individuals who are considered to be agents of institutional change. By reviewing the five case studies representing practice in corresponding countries and looking at the systematic comparison of these practices, readers are exposed to a range of mandates in faculty/educational development units and the strategies and practices each uses. The second section of this book may help readers structure their own professional development by reflecting on what they do and whether their expertise and know-how matches the tasks at hand, the extent to which their practice is evidence-based, and ways in which they can determine the effectiveness and impact of their work.

A second group of stakeholders for whom the book would be of interest is policymakers. They will find in this book the potential power of educational development and realize how they can partner with educational developers to address the challenges they face, particularly with respect to enhancing quality and engaging in quality assurance. The comparative chapter is also of particular interest to them as it elaborates how faculty development policies in higher education institutions reflect modes of regulation. Finally, they will obtain a more coherent picture of how the field is evolving and thus can benchmark their institutional practice internationally and, in doing so, help build the teaching and learning capacity of their institution.

Faculty and teaching staff will also benefit from reading this book because it will help them develop an understanding of the importance of their own initial and continuing training and professional development and how this plays out in other countries. They will also discover the centrality of their role in the partnership for educational development.

Researchers in higher education can benefit from the book by gaining a more profound understanding of the field of educational development and the need for a reliable body of cumulative evidence to inform a wide range of practices.

Finally, graduate students will have an overview of the current state of faculty development in five countries and how the field may be conceptualized. This may help them find a niche for their own professional development as academics, educational developers, and researchers in higher education.

The Structure of the Book

The bulk of the book (parts one and two) comprises chapters written by the original members of the FACDEV Mobility Project. The prologue and epilogue are invited international contributions and, in addition to broadening the perspective offered in the book, enhance its multicultural and international flavor.

James Groccia, a U.S. specialist on educational leadership development and the former president of the Professional and Organizational Development Network (POD), the main professional organization for educational developers in the United States, provides an insightful perspective in the prologue about faculty development in light of global changes. Because of the complexity of our times, he proposes a multidimensional approach to faculty development that would address issues pertaining to organizational and personal development, assessment, the effective use of technology, curriculum organization, and classroom instruction. This chapter sets the scene for introducing international practices of faculty and educational development, offered in part one. In part one, five case studies present descriptive and interpretative accounts of faculty development practices and contexts in Canada (Taylor and Bédard), Switzerland (Rege Colet), Denmark (Kolmos), Belgium (Clement and Frenay), and France (Paul and Adangnikou). Their accounts are rich and diverse as they represent varied cultural and linguistic contexts (English, Dutch, Danish, and French), both among and within countries (Canada with anglophone and francophone cultures and Belgium with Flemish and French communities). They also represent centralized/

decentralized modes of governments with different funding and accountability implications and centralized/decentralized faculty/educational development units.

The first case study recounts the long history of faculty development in Canada and the current contextual factors contributing to the development of the field. It provides an overview of structures and programs across the country and discusses some of the challenges that are bound to shape the future of faculty development practice and its scholarship.

The chapter on faculty development in Switzerland examines how the political context and the fight for autonomy have led Swiss universities to develop support centers for teaching in higher education. It outlines the circumstances that have supported the growth of centers and tackles the question of defining faculty development in a multicultural and multilingual environment.

In Denmark, pedagogical staff development is compulsory and, as to appointment at the assistant professor level, contingent on formal pedagogical qualifications. The chapter highlights advantages and disadvantages of the nationally decentralized Danish faculty development strategies and points out how Danish development centers are structured and the relevance of educational developer networks within this context. Elaboration of the specific case of Aalborg University helps to explain how national policies are put into practice.

The chapter on faculty development in Belgian universities provides a general overview of the structure and characteristics of Belgian higher education and describes how faculty development is conceptualized and enacted in Flanders and in the French-speaking community.

The France case study is unique in that it describes a situation where faculty development has not flourished at all. Why does France distinguish itself from other countries in this regard? Why do French universities remain on the sidelines of changes? By explaining the rules and regulations, the institutional context and epistemology, the authors conclude that, in this decade, the demands of the Bologna process concerning quality, combined with demographic changes in student and faculty profiles, provide a more accommodating climate for advancing the concept and practice of faculty development in France.

While each chapter paints the details of a specific context and practice, together they convey a clear message concerning the significance of policy in changing practice in general and the practice of faculty and educational development in particular. We learn that these changes can be at the meso level, as is the case with the Bologna process and the impact it is having on quality assurance mechanisms, including within faculty development. They can be at the macro or national level, as in Denmark, or they can be at the micro or institutional level, as in Canada and Belgium.

Following the five case studies, chapter 6 (Frenay and Saroyan) offers a systematic comparison of faculty/educational development practices, highlighting divergences and convergences and discussing the influence of national and institutional policies on shaping the mandate of educational/faculty development units and their respective practices. One insight gained from this comparison is the role of regulatory bodies and their influence on higher education systems and how these can influence the organizational structure and development of faculty development units.

The second part is the outcome of an analytic and synthesizing exercise leading to the conceptualization of our shared practice of and research in educational development. Although coauthored by two individuals (Taylor and Rege Colet), it is fair to say that this chapter (7) and the next (Bédard, Clement, and Taylor) are the fruits of a collective effort of making the tacit explicit and putting it to the test. Chapter 7 represents a meta-analysis of educational development practice and its multiple dimensions across contexts. The result is a concrete concept map, a tool that can inform educational developers in their work. Chapter 8 describes our attempts to validate this tool with faculty developers during three international professional conferences.

Kirsten Hofgaard Lycke, former president of the International Consortium for Educational Development (ICED) and a leader in educational development in Scandinavian countries, wrote the epilogue. She provides an analytic view of the chapters and places their contribution within the context of a more global view of educational development and its position in this changing higher education landscape. More important, she challenges all of us to think about more innovative approaches to advance our discipline with respect to both theory and practice.

We hope that you enjoy reading this book as much as we enjoyed producing it, and that it becomes the stimulus for furthering the development of the theoretical and practical base for faculty and educational development.

Notes

1. By the end of the Mobility Project, a total of 40 students were able to benefit: 19 Canadians spent one month in Europe, and 21 Europeans spent one month in Canada.

2. Ten team members of the participating universities were able to teach in another university during the project: five Canadians went to Europe; five Europeans went to Canada.

3. The lead at the University of Manitoba was Dr. K. Lynn Taylor, who has since changed her institution and is currently the Director of the Centre for Learning and Teaching at Dalhousie University in Halifax, Nova Scotia, Canada.

4. The overarching aim of the Bologna process is to create the European Higher Education Area (EHEA) based on international cooperation and academic exchange that is attractive to European students and staff as well as to students and staff from other parts of the world. (Definition source: http://www.ond.vlaanderen.be/hoger onderwijs/bologna/).

References

Bransford, J. P., Stevens, R., Schwartz, D., Meltzoff, A., Pea, R., Roschelle, J., Vye, N., Kuhl, P., Barron, B., Reeves, B., & Sabelli, N. (2006). Learning theories of education: Toward a decade of synergy. In P. Alexander & P. Winnie (Eds.), *Handbook of educational psychology* (2nd ed., pp. 209–244). Mahwah, NJ: Laurence Erlbaum.

Frenay, M., Saroyan, A., Clement, M., Kolmos, A., Paul, J.-J., Bédard, D., Taylor, L., & Rege Colet, N. (2005). *FACDEV Program: Promoting faculty development to enhance the quality of learning in higher education*. Bruxelles, Belgium: European Union, DG Education and Culture.

Rowland, S. (1999). The role of theory in a pedagogical model for lecturers in higher education. *Studies in Higher Education, 24*, 303–314.

WHY FACULTY DEVELOPMENT?
WHY NOW?

James Groccia

Before addressing the questions of the prologue's title, I must first discuss terminology. My use of the term faculty development *throughout this chapter represents the prevalent U.S. perspective on the work with the common goal "to develop the potential of the existing resources and structures of institutions by viewing and using them in creative ways. These resources include the faculty and staff, the courses and programs, all of which can become self-renewing once we become aware of the possibilities" (Professional and Organizational Network in Higher Education [POD], 2002). Subsumed in this term is a multidimensional focus on the faculty member as a teacher, scholar, professional, and person; on the course and curriculum and student learning; and on the organizational structure of the institution and its subcomponents. Faculty development is not used universally to represent this type of work, however. Other terms used in other countries include* educational development, academic development, instructional development, *and* staff development.

Preparing to Deal With Critical Global Issues

The quality of higher education and the need to facilitate high-level learning has never been more important. As the world continues to shrink (becoming "flatter," according to Thomas Friedman), the result of economic interdependence, global competition, and expanding communication technology, tertiary or higher education becomes more critical for all countries around the world (Friedman, 2007, p. 289). As Rischard (2002) states, the new world economy is highly knowledge-intensive, and one must be good at constantly learning—if one stands still, one falls back (p. 30). Higher education plays a central role in finding solutions to what Rischard sees as the critical global issues facing future generations worldwide. These two writers highlight the possibility (probability?) that what goes on inside the world's higher-education classrooms has a profound impact on more than an individual student's grades; global economic and social success and even worldwide survival may rest in the balance.

Becoming More Relevant

According to the Association of American Colleges and Universities (AAC& U, 2007), higher education stands at a crossroads where millions of students are entering a higher-education system that requires a recalibration of teaching methods and learning outcomes to face the demands of new global realities. To be most relevant to this new world, higher education must recognize and attain essential learning outcomes that integrate liberal education values, methods, and content across the entire spectrum of academic disciplines. As the world is reshaped by scientific and technological innovations, global interdependence, cross-cultural contacts, and changes in economic and political power balances, the goals of higher education must also change (AAC& U, 2007). In the face of these shifting future realities, we must support faculty to initiate curricular changes that prepare all students for new 21st-century challenges by gaining

- knowledge of human cultures and the physical and natural world through study in the sciences, mathematics, social sciences, humanities, histories, languages, and the arts;
- intellectual and practical abilities, including inquiry and analysis, critical and creative thinking, written and oral communication, quantitative and information literacy, teamwork, and problem-solving skills by engagement with big, timely, and enduring questions;
- personal and social responsibility, including civic knowledge and engagement, intercultural knowledge and competence, ethical reasoning and action, and foundations and skills for lifelong learning that

is practiced across the curriculum through challenging problems and projects; and

- integrative learning, including synthesis and advanced study across both general and specialized study demonstrated through the application of knowledge, skills, and responsibilities to new settings and complex problems (AAC&U, 2007).

Each of these essential learning outcomes requires higher-education faculty to develop effective educational practices that engage students across disciplinary boundaries in active learning that tackles real problems and leads to sustained intellectual growth, results that can be applied realistically, and a heightened sense of personal responsibility. The AAC&U report (2007) calls on educational leaders to "expand substantially investments in active, hands-on, collaborative, and inquiry-based forms of teaching and learning— making full use of new educational technologies—to ensure that all students have rich opportunities" to achieve learning goals essential for the new global century (AAC&U, 2007, p. 11). Furthermore, the use of effective and engaging educational practices, the central goal of faculty development practices and teaching and learning centers, is proposed as the key to higher achievement for contemporary and future college students (AAC&U, 2007).

Today's university students are being asked to respond to a rapidly changing world with interdependent judgments and decisions that blend theoretical, practical, professional, and moral foundations. To be most effective, higher education must combine liberal-education and professional-education orientations to provide students with access to solutions to pressing human problems based on reflective intellectual practices by reconnecting analytic insight with practical judgment and action (Sullivan & Rosin, 2008). According to Sullivan and Rosin, higher education must better prepare students for lives of engagement and responsibility overcoming the traditional tension and separation between liberal arts (*life of the mind*) and professional education (*life of practice*). To do this, Sullivan and Rosin state that faculty must be supported to meet and overcome developmental, institutional, dialogical, and contextual challenges. To overcome developmental challenges, faculty members need support to engage in collaborative relationships based on dialogue, communication, and reflection to discover the meaning of teaching for practical judgment. To meet institutional challenges, we must support faculty and administrative leaders to integrate individual, disciplinary, and institutional needs to find relationships between campus-based teaching and practical contexts and outcomes. Supporting faculty to serve as exemplars, mentors, and models can address dialogic and contextual challenges by providing opportunities for faculty to see commonalities across disciplinary perspectives to find shared purpose. Faculty development programs and teaching and learning centers are ideal places for the support needed to overcome these challenges.

Focusing on Productivity and Quality

Higher education throughout the world is facing a crisis that cannot be solved by making minor changes to the same old ways of doing things. On the most visible level, this crisis manifests itself in fiscal terms: ever-rising student tuition, decreasing public funding for higher-education budgets, and shrinking investments in tenure-track faculty. On a less visible but perhaps more important level, this crisis is evidenced by increased calls for accountability and an escalating loss of trust in and rising skepticism about the value of higher education.

According to the National Center for Educational Statistics ([NCES], 2007), for the 2006–2007 academic year, annual costs for undergraduate tuition, room, and board at U.S. higher education institutions were estimated to be $11,034 at public institutions and $28,384 at private institutions. Between 1996–1997 and 2006–2007, costs for undergraduate tuition, room, and board at public higher education institutions rose by 32%, and at private institutions by 22% (after adjustments for inflation). During the same period, consumer prices rose by 28%. The net cost of attending college grew at a faster rate than both median income and disposable per capita income during the 1980s and 1990s at all types of higher-education institutions in the United States (NCES, 2002). Adding to the problem of rising costs is the added debt burden students and parents must shoulder as they try to finance college education. An even more important impact for the future is the reduction in access to higher education for students with limited financial means.

A major factor driving student costs higher is the decline in state and federal support for higher education in the United States. Provincial government support and tuition income have traditionally accounted for 90% of operating revenues for Canadian higher-education institutions (Association of Universities and Colleges of Canada [AUCC], 2008). The sources of this funding have shifted dramatically over the past 26 years, however. In 1980, 84% of the funding for teaching and unsponsored research costs came from government sources, student fees (tuition) provided about 10%, and returns on investments and donations accounted for the remainder. By 2006, the figures indicated less government support (66%) and, correspondingly, increased reliance on student fees (24%) and returns on investments and donations (10%).

Corresponding to a reduction in (provincial and state) government support is an increased reliance on student tuition and fees. For example, for the period between the 1996–1997 and 2002–2003 academic years, the proportion of Auburn University's budget from tuition and fees increased from 18% to almost 30%—a whopping 56% jump! Fueled by economic recession, declining tax revenues, and priorities shifting toward homeland security and health care, state budget declines have forced many universities to institute deep spending cuts.

There have been similar decreases in government support for higher education in Canada. Per student provincial government funding in Canada fell from $17,900 in 1980–1981 to $9,900 in 2006–2007. When comparing the United States to Canada, in terms of per student funding for higher education, we find interesting trends. Funding patterns for higher education in Canada compared to those in the United States show declining per student funding, a marked shift in the advantage once held by Canadian higher education. This funding advantage began to evaporate in the latter part of the 1980s and has reversed to the point that U.S. public universities now have more than an $8,000 per student advantage (AUCC, 2008). This means that Canadian public universities have even smaller investment opportunities than do U.S. institutions, including investment in full-time faculty. The growth of full-time faculty in Canada has not been able to match the equivalent growth in full-time student enrollment. While the latter grew by 56% between 1987 and 2006, the former increased by only 18% during the same period (AUCC, 2008).

As McNeil (2008) points out, government cutbacks and increased reliance on student tuition is truly a worldwide phenomenon:

> The situation has become more critical in recent years as public support of higher education has shrunk. Both the elite national universities, which receive the bulk of federal higher-education funds, and the regional public

universities, which get their money from municipal governments, or prefectures, have become increasingly dependent on tuition. (p. A17)

In June 2005, the *New York Times* reported on the impact of recent changes to the U.S. Federal Financial Aid funding formula on increasing the cost for attending college and its impact on upward mobility, an aspect of the American experience that has been a magnet for generations of immigrants (my own father and grandparents included). By increasing the amount of money families must contribute to the cost of education before they are eligible for federal and state financial aid, the United States is

> rapidly abandoning a long-standing policy aimed at keeping college afford-able for all Americans who qualify academically. . . . [The United States] as a whole has been disinvesting in higher education at a time when college has become crucial to workforce participation and to the nation's ability to meet the challenges of global competition. . . . Until the country renews its commitment to making college affordable for everyone, the American dream of upward mobility through education will be in danger of dying out. (*"Crushing Upward Mobility,"* 2005)

The picture becomes even more dire when one considers the limited fiscal resources for higher education in developing countries, where there is even less room for wasting effort, time, and money. Teaching and learning quality is not an option, but it may be becoming a luxury that students and governments cannot afford; one could argue that it is a requirement if developing countries want to be simply beneficiaries of, never mind contributors to, the burgeoning knowledge economy.

Higher education in the United States has shifted dramatically away from hiring full-time faculty toward employing part-time academics. The U.S. Education Department reports that in 2005 only slightly more than half (52%) of higher-education faculty were full-time employees, a sharp reduction from the 66% full-time faculty reported in 1987 ("The 2007–2008 Almanac," 2007). This trend threatens the traditional fabric of the higher-education community and can have negative effects on student success and retention. According to the briefing paper of the Greater Expectations National Panel on the use and impact of part-time faculty in higher education, part-time faculty are often less available to students and less able to participate in institutional activities (Miller, 2001). This report quotes Jane

Buck, then president of the American Association of University Professors (AAUP), as saying that, as a result of decreased contact time, part-time faculty may reduce the quality of student learning by avoiding labor-intensive writing assignments to save grading time, self-censoring classroom discussions in the absence of academic freedom protections, avoiding rigorous assessments and/or inflating grades to boost student evaluations, and pandering to students to build popularity and help ensure continued employment (Miller, 2001).

While higher-education institutions in other parts of the world have not experienced the shift from full- to part-time faculty to the same extent as the United States, the increase in full-time instructional staff has not kept up with the increase in student enrollment. In both the UK and Australia the ratio of full-time faculty has not kept pace with equivalent full-time student enrollment increases. In the UK, from the mid-1990s to the mid-2000s, student enrollment grew by 25%, while the number of full-time faculty grew by only 20%. Since 1995 full-time student enrollment in Australia has grown by 41%, while full-time faculty has increased by only 10% (AUCC, 2008).

Paralleling the decline in financial support for higher education has been a decline in public trust, leading to rising skepticism about the quality and future of colleges and universities. Under the general term of "accountability," governing bodies and public groups are increasingly asking for evidence of higher education's impact. In the United States, federal and state governing agencies have adopted political and financial agendas that challenge higher education's perceived fiscal irresponsibility, autonomy, goals, and values. Rightly or wrongly, parents and students appear to believe that colleges are expensive and wasteful. The public seems to be growing increasingly dissatisfied with higher education's perceived lack of interest in teaching due to increasing emphasis on research, publication, and disciplinary specialization, of which the relevance to student welfare has been called into question (Boyer Commission on Educating Undergraduates in the Research University, 1998).

Criticism of the academy comes from within as well. Derek Bok (2006), former president of Harvard University, surveyed current research on higher education's success in attaining commonly accepted goals of undergraduate education and concludes that colleges and universities come up short. Despite increased curricular offerings, expansion of educational services and added cumulative resources over the past half-century, powerful educational technology, and new curricula, there is little hard evidence that our students learn more than they did 50 years ago. Bok calls for increased attention to improved teaching, more student engagement in learning, and higher-quality faculty development to revitalize U.S. higher education.

The National Center for Public Policy and Higher Education (NCP PHE), in its review of worldwide educational statistics, provides evidence that U.S. higher education, compared to that in other countries, may also be underachieving. The United States ranks 16th out of 27 developed countries studied in this report in the percentage of students who complete their first undergraduate degree. The inescapable fact outlined in this and previous reports by NCPPHE is that American higher education is underperforming and is being outperformed by many other countries (NCPPHE, 2006)

Faculty Development: Part of the Solution

There is no simple, single solution to this situation. We must encourage creative thinking that places a priority on a top-to-bottom focus on quality, where every aspect of institutional functioning is analyzed. The growth of faculty development services is a hopeful sign for educational quality: after centuries of stagnation in the traditional, efficient, but less effective lecture mode, faculty development activities are helping higher education in a slow but persistent evolution from a teaching to a learning paradigm. In light of the mounting pressures just described, higher education's future may depend on continuing a unified campuswide effort to develop innovative approaches to increasing teaching and learning quality, and on supporting institutional efforts to develop policies and procedures that enhance faculty success along research and service dimensions.

Faculty development must take a multidimensional approach that includes six distinct yet interrelated approaches to increasing quality teaching and learning: organizational development, assessment, personal development, technology use, curricular organization, and classroom instruction (Groccia & Miller, 2005). Faculty development can improve learning quality by focusing attention on one or more of these areas.

Organizational Development

Faculty development can support efforts to increase quality by engaging in organizational strategies that take a big-picture perspective, focusing on institutional planning and transformation. Operational inefficiencies and organizational redundancies must be minimized, and strategic planning—as opposed to the common approach to academic leadership, which could be labeled advancement by "random acts of progress"—must provide direction for innovation and must actually be followed (Franz & Morrison, 2005). Organizational development activities could also include advocacy efforts on behalf of teaching and learning or policymaking related to academic leadership development, faculty performance, assessment, and work life realities.

Assessment

Faculty development organizations must help institutions implement assessment strategies that rest on valid and reliable uses of measurement. Such organizations must adopt a culture of assessment to demonstrate the impact of academic programs and instructional activities (including scholarship of teaching and learning research) and the development of effective grading practices tied to institutional goals. Instructional effort and faculty time as well as the allocation of university resources must be measured regularly against the attainment of desired institutional, faculty, and student learning outcomes. Assessment can also relate to evaluation of faculty performance related to academic functions and measurement of the effectiveness and impact of faculty development activities.

Personal Development

Institutions must renew their focus on personal faculty development, with increased attention to mentoring and training current and future faculty for work that is actually done (which is primarily teaching) and for understanding the interrelationships among cost, effort, and quality. The impending retirement of large numbers of faculty in the United States, Canada, and other parts of the world reinforces the need for faculty development activities that focus on pipeline issues to recruit, develop, and mentor the next generation of instructional staff. The personal development of faculty in our changing world, where expectations for higher standards of teaching, research, and service are increasingly ratcheted up, is of critical importance (Massy, Wilger, & Colbeck, 1994). Additionally, increased pressure by institutions, government agencies, and the general public to demonstrate positive student learning outcomes as well as the need to respond to changes in student demographics have contributed to heightened stress on faculty lives. The increase in the number of female faculty members has also contributed to the need to develop human-friendly personnel policies (for example, tenure clock stoppage and family leave) and work supports (for example, child care facilities) that have distinctly personal dimensions.

Technology Use

Learning and teaching quality can also be enhanced by using technology appropriately and for the right reasons. Faculty development units play a central role in supporting technology use. Technology can also focus attention on course design and delivery principles that are embedded in and supported by robust learning theories and research. This second-order impact of technology can guide and assist in creating effective learning environments, instructional development activities, and teaching, even if technology itself is not used in instruction. While not a panacea, technology can increase access to information and to students and can have a positive impact on costs and quality.

Curricular Organization

Higher-education institutions, with assistance from faculty development units, can increase learning through curricular reform. Faculty members, department chairs, and deans must be supported in carefully investigating what is taught and when it is taught to keep curriculum relevant and to reduce unnecessary content repetition and redundancy. Curricular development can take place at the individual faculty member level or on a departmental scale. An example of the latter is the innovations taking place in Denmark, which is institutionalizing problem-based learning (PBL) in engineering departments across the spectrum of national institutions (Hansen & Du, 2004). This type of curricular development requires intensive support and assistance from faculty development units at all levels: introducing concepts; designing courses; developing teaching, evaluation, and assessment skills; and providing feedback and program revision services.

Classroom Instruction

Faculty development experts must support colleges and universities to challenge and support their instructional staff to use effective, evidence-based classroom teaching strategies to increase learning productivity and quality. Integral to the use of evidence to improve classroom instruction is agreement about what constitutes evidence of quality. Faculty development units can initiate campus-based discussion of quality and how to measure it accurately.

Faculty Development Experience in the United States

The founding of a national network for faculty development and faculty developers, which eventually became the Professional and Organizational Network in Higher Education (POD), is described by Joan North and Stephen Scholl (1979). POD can trace its roots to national efforts by foundations such as Kellogg, Lilly, and Danforth and agencies such as the Fund for the Improvement of Postsecondary Education (FIPSE) to fund projects "devoted to the renewal of institutions through 'faculty development,' especially the improvement of instruction" (North & Scholl, 1979, p. 10). These efforts were not revolutionary but evolutionary, as programs and initiatives were stirring in the 1940s, '50s, and '60s in individual colleges and universities to provide assistance with the evaluation of teaching, the use of audiovisual aids, professional renewal, and curriculum development (Gaff, 1975; Gaff & Simpson, 1994; Graf, Albright, & Wheeler, 1992; Group for Human Development in Higher Education, 1974; Lewis, 1996; North & Scholl, 1979). By 1975, Gaff was able to identify 218 faculty development programs or centers in the United States.

The creation of programs to improve teaching and learning during the late 1960s and early '70s was energized by student protests for improved quality and curricular relevance; the prospects of leveling student enrollments; stagnation of faculty mobility; increased access and student diversity; and increased dissemination of new research results on teaching, learning, and instructional methodology (Gaff, 1978). The mid-1970s were a time of energized activities in support of faculty development, and seminal publications and meetings abounded. However, the midpoint of the 1970s was not all cheery as many states and institutions experienced financial difficulties, which in some cases led to faculty retrenchment. These two trends led to conferences and meetings on the need to organize some kind of national network, which resulted in the founding of POD in 1979.

In 2008 POD's membership exceeded 1,800 (more than 10% from outside the United States and Canada), making it the world's largest organization dedicated to enhancing learning through faculty, instructional, and educational development. Almost one-third of all four-year U.S. colleges and universities are currently represented by membership in POD, up from less than one-quarter in 2004. According to its website (http://www.podnetwork.org/about.htm.), POD's mission is to foster human development in higher education through faculty, instructional, and organizational development. POD believes that the development of students is a fundamental purpose of higher education and requires for its success effective advising, teaching, leadership, and management. Central to POD's philosophy is lifelong, holistic, personal, and professional learning; growth; and change for the higher-education community. To promote faculty development, POD provides support and services for its members through publications, conferences, consulting, and networking; offers services and resources to others interested in faculty development; and plays an advocacy role nationally and internationally in seeking to inform and persuade educational leaders of the value of faculty, instructional, and organizational development in institutions of higher education.

While the presence of faculty development efforts in institutions of higher education in the United States (and in the other countries profiled in this book) has grown steadily during the last 30 years, has sufficient support been garnered for what higher education is about—the creation, diffusion, and dissemination of knowledge? Has sufficient support been garnered for those who make this all happen—our instructional staff, graduate students, support personnel, and administrators? When we look at other sectors with regard to the level of support provided for what I will call professional development, the answers to these questions may be no.

According to 2003 data published by the American Society for Training and Development (ASTD), U.S. companies annually spend on average between 2% and 3% of payroll and invest about 24 hours per employee on professional development (Cowart, Hetzel, & Trosley, 2003). *Training* magazine's Top 50 companies spend on average almost 4% of payroll and provide 66 hours per employee for training each year. This translates to between $300 and $1,500 per employee annually. Most of these companies spend about half of their training dollars on content development, 8% to 10% on infrastructure, and the remaining 40% to 50% on salaries and facilities (Bersin, 2003). As *Training* magazine indicates, "In the training and development world, the best learning organizations are far from static. These companies are continually developing innovative programs that develop and stimulate their organization's human capital" (Johnson, 2004, p. 42). When it comes to professional development, the corporate sector in the United States (and I suspect in other parts of the world), is "putting its money where its mouth is." To use another common expression, when it comes to training and efforts to improve performance and outcomes, U.S. business is "walking the walk, not just talking the talk."

Can these levels of support for professional development in the corporate sector be compared with higher education's expenditures for faculty development? This is a question to which the answer is all the more important when one takes into account that most faculty have not had even basic training in pedagogy, which for most comprises at least 50% of what they do (that is, teaching). Unfortunately, I cannot answer with any degree of certainty as few data are available to reliably summarize what each of our institutions individually, and higher education collectively, spend on faculty development. My best response is to ask more questions for personal reflection and investigation: Does your institution have a unit dedicated to professional development, and what is its mission and overall budget? What is your professional development budget? How much does this translate to per instructional staff member? What incentives do you provide to faculty to participate in professional development activities? What percentage of your institution's total budget does your budget represent? While these questions may be difficult to answer, they are no less important to ask, and this book may provide a needed stimulus for beginning this investigation.

Researching and Publicizing Faculty Development Effectiveness

The corporate sector's expenditures for professional development may be understood more readily because it may be easier to relate professional development directly to changes in employee performance and corporate outcomes (profits). The connections between faculty development and improvement in instruction and learning and between student and faculty retention and success, assuming that these are intended outcomes of our work, are more difficult to establish. Those responsible for faculty development on each and every campus should strive to make these connections clear through rigorous, well-designed research and widespread dissemination of results. Additionally, there is a role for faculty developers to contribute to broad-based discussion on what constitutes quality teaching, how to measure it, and how to assess its impact on student learning.

It is easier to show a positive relationship between professional development and improvements in teaching. It is more difficult to go the next step and show that faculty development leads directly to better learning. Prebble et al. (2005) have researched the connection between faculty and educational development and improvements in teaching and student learning. They conclude:

> The relationship between what teachers do and what students learn is complex. There are many variables that may affect student outcomes. There is virtually no research on any direct relationship between academic staff development and student learning outcomes. Rather it is an indirect, two-step relationship—academic staff development programs can improve teaching, and good teaching contributes to good student outcomes (as measured by retention, persistence, and achievement). (p. 2)

Faculty can be assisted to improve the quality of teaching through the kind of activities that faculty development offices provide, and good teaching can be shown to have positive affects on student learning outcomes. According to this research synthesis and other reports (Gibbs & Coffey, 2004; Ho, Watkins, & Kelly, 2001; Polich, 2008; Postareff, Lindblom-Ylänne, & Nevgi, 2007; Rust, 1998; Stes, Clement, & Van Petegem, 2007), faculty development works to change teaching behavior. However, more evidence must be gathered to assess the direct impact of improved teaching on student learning and/or other measures of educational quality.

The Need for a Scholarship of Practice

Stimulated by Boyer (1990), Hutchings and Shulman (1999), and others, faculty development programs have assisted faculty in broadening their definitions of scholarship and in conducting scholarship of teaching and learning. In this discourse one often hears of a continuum from scholarly teaching to scholarship of teaching. Faculty development professionals may want to adopt this continuum metaphor and think about their work as spanning a continuum from scholarly faculty development to scholarship of faculty development. Faculty developers need to approach what they do as meaningful intellectual work that builds on sound scholarship of learning, human behavior, teaching, organizational structure and behavior, and disciplinary and academic culture. We need to nurture an active scholarship of practice that has the same clarity and precision as is sought in scholarship of teaching and learning, and that has traditionally been applied to work within our own academic fields. In this way, faculty developers can add to the literature to build a stronger foundation for the impact of faculty development on teaching and student learning to bolster the call for increased support, recognition, and reward.

The Need for Clarity of Pathways Into the Faculty Development Profession

To maintain the progress and consequence that faculty development has achieved worldwide collectively and individually, we need to incorporate a serious investigation of what it means to be a profession into and among each national faculty development organization. Clarifying and agreeing on competencies, attitudes, values, abilities, and knowledge base underpinning faculty development needs to be on each national faculty development agenda. While some countries—a few of which are described in this book— have made progress in identifying these skills for faculty and academic professionals, few have attempted to develop a scheme for determining what it means to be a professional faculty developer, and fewer still have developed clear pathways for entering this line of work. The question that begs an answer is: Can we expect others—faculty, graduate and undergraduate students, administrators—to seek our assistance, to risk their security and perhaps their careers, by following our suggestions, if we cannot clearly articulate and demonstrate some competence or level of expertise? By not doing so, we risk hearing the common critique of teaching, that "anyone can teach; after all, I've spent my life as a learner exposed to teachers" being applied as well to faculty developers, that "anyone can do faculty development; after all, I've spent my career teaching."

Faculty development, at least in the United States, has blossomed in part because what has been and is being done is open to all or most within the academy who have secured some level of credibility. In addition, in no way do I want to denigrate the good work that has been and is being done. Doing faculty development work most often has been a voluntary choice based on commitment to learning, teaching, students, and departments or institutions; some even refer to it as a calling. Flexibility and a shared sense of democracy allow us to do this teaching and learning. However, as David Hume, a faculty development colleague from the UK once said to me, "If we don't take ourselves seriously, why should anyone else?" Taking ourselves

seriously means developing standards, competencies, credentialing procedures, and ongoing opportunities for continuous professional development.
I doubt that one would go to a dentist or a pharmacist or entrust children
to a primary school teacher without the training and qualifications that indicate a level of competence and expertise. Faculty developers cannot continue
to expect that faculty and instructional staff will simply trust us and, similarly, expect that our employers will provide us with a portion of their limited funds to have a positive impact on student learning without a similar
process to enter and remain in the profession. While there has been marked
progress in credentialing faculty developers through the development of fel-
lowship schemes by the Staff and Educational Development Association
(SEDA) in the UK and The Higher Education Research and Development
Society of Australasia (HERDSA) in Australia and New Zealand, much still
needs be done, especially in the United States.

Expanding the Knowledge of Others Through Faculty Development

Faculty developers must become increasingly responsive to the changing face
of faculty and students and the changing nature of academic work life realities around the world. While some progress has been made in recognizing
the increasing diversity among student populations, faculty development has
not done as well in understanding and responding to the corresponding
shifts in faculty and international higher education. As Hutchings, Huber,
and Golde (2006) have written, we must begin to think differently about
faculty careers. Efforts to integrate "work" and "life" will be more pressing
in the future. As these authors point out, the large group of faculty members
hired in the United States during the 1960s and '70s is rapidly approaching
retirement. The new generation replacing them will look different and will
require work and life conditions that are flexible and balanced.

According to the National Survey of Postsecondary Faculty published
by the National Center for Educational Statistics in 1999 (cited in American
Council on Education Office of Women in Higher Education, 2005), 90%
of full-time faculty members 20 years ago were White males. Today, women
earn more than half of the doctorates given to U.S. citizens by American

universities and represent almost 40% of full-time faculty, while 15% of full-time faculty are people of color. Published by the American Council on Education in 2005, *An Agenda for Excellence: Creating Flexibility in Tenure-Track Faculty Careers* challenges higher education to assess and address the institutional climate that governs the entire career cycle for new faculty. Further, it states that universities must create more flexible career paths for tenure-track faculty to enter, thrive in, and retire from academe. Those of us in faculty development must think and plan new strategies that will help facilitate this new professoriate's success. We are often on the front line of this process, and these efforts certainly fall in both the faculty and the organizational development components of our organization. I do not know whether the countries profiled in this book are experiencing similar changes in their instructional staff. However, I do suspect that faculty development worldwide should be cognizant of shifts in faculty as they represent the core target group for faculty development efforts.

Faculty development efforts must be sensitive to institutional and national context. The form and focus of faculty development efforts must reflect the needs and priorities of individual institutions and nations. From a global perspective, developing countries may very well require the nurturing and development of faculty research skills in parallel with (or even in preference to) teaching skills. Faculty development activities can legitimately address this need.

The need exists to continue to reach out to others within the worldwide higher education community, to parlay our expertise and energy with others in joint efforts to enhance teaching, learning, institutional change, and faculty development. This is a big job and one that will surely benefit from strong and mutually supportive partnerships. Faculty developers must work to understand and support the work of others; to mentor others; and, in turn, to be mentored in this process. This book is one step in this direction, a guide to understanding something about the history and culture of faculty development internationally.

Faculty developers will benefit from what others around the world can share. Through this understanding, we are able to move beyond the boundaries of our institutions, our states, and our nations toward the creation of a true international community of scholars, an international network of faculty development. The world in which we live deserves no less.

References

American Council on Education Office of Women in Higher Education. (2005). *An agenda for excellence: Creating flexibility in tenure-track faculty careers*. Retrieved from www.acenet.edu/bookstore/pdf/2005_tenure_flex_summary.pdf.

Association of American Colleges and Universities (AAC&U). (2007). *College learning for the new global century: A report from the national leadership council for liberal education & America's promise*. Retrieved from http://www.hivcampus education.org/LEAP/documents/GlobalCentury_final.pdf.

Association of Universities and Colleges of Canada (AUCC). (2008). *Trends in higher education: Vol. 3. Finance*. Ottawa, Canada: Author.

Bersin, J. (2003). *Training analytics: The next big wave in learning management technology*. Retrieved from http://www.clomedia.com/content/anmviewer.asp?a=325& print=yes.

Bok, D. C. (2006). *Our underachieving colleges: A candid look at how much students learn and why they should be learning more*. Princeton, NJ: Princeton University.

Boyer Commission on Educating Undergraduates in the Research University. (1998). *Reinventing undergraduate education: A blueprint for America's research universities*. Retrieved from http://naples.cc.sunysb.edu/pres/boyer.nsf/673918 d46fbf653e852565ec0056ff3e/d955b61ffddd590a852565ec005717ae/$FILE/boyer .pdf.

Boyer, E. L. (1990). *Scholarship reconsidered: Priorities of the professoriate*. Princeton, NJ: The Carnegie Foundation for the Advancement of Teaching.

Cowart, F., Hetzel, D. R., & Trosley, S. A. (2003). *The Committed Newspaper*. Retrieved from http://www.asne.org/index.cfm?ID=4931.

Crushing upward mobility [Electronic version]. (2005, June 7). *New York Times*. Retrieved from http://www.nytimes.com/2005/06/07/opinion/07tues2.html? scp=50&sq=2005/06/07&st=cse.

Franz, L. S., & Morrison, D. R. (2005). Random acts of progress versus planned productivity via strategic planning. In J. Groccia & J. E. Miller (Eds.), *On becoming a productive university: Strategies for reducing costs and increasing quality in higher education* (pp. 14–22). Bolton, MA: Anker.

Friedman, T. (2007). *The world is flat 3.0: A brief history of the twenty-first century*. New York: Picador.

Gaff, J. G. (1975). *Toward faculty renewal: Advances in faculty, instructional, and organizational development*. San Francisco, CA: Jossey-Bass.

Gaff, J. G. (1978). Editors' note. In J. G. Gaff (Ed.), *New directions for higher education: Vol. 24. Institutional renewal through the improvement of teaching* (pp. vii–xi). San Francisco, CA: Jossey-Bass.

Gaff, J. G., & Simpson, R. D. (1994). Faculty development in the United States. *Innovative Higher Education, 18*(3), 167–176.

Gibbs, G., & Coffey, M. (2004). The impact of training of university teachers on their teaching skills, their approach to teaching and the approach to learning of their students. *Active Learning in Higher Education, 5*(1), 87–100.

Graf, D. L., Albright, M. J., & Wheeler, D. W. (1992). Faculty development's role in improving undergraduate education. In M. J. Albright & D. L. Graf (Eds.), *New directions for teaching and learning: Vol. 51. Teaching in the information age: The role of educational technology* (pp. 101–109). San Francisco, CA: Jossey-Bass.

Groccia, J., & Miller, J. E. (2005). *On becoming a productive university: Strategies for reducing costs and increasing quality in higher education.* Bolton, MA: Anker.

Group for Human Development in Higher Education. (1974). *Faculty development in a time of retrenchment.* New Rochelle, NY: Change Magazine.

Hansen, S., & Du, X. (2004). *Integrating international students into a project-organized problem-based learning environment.* Retrieved from http://people .plan.aau.dk/~sh/Publikationer/PaperWCETE'2004.pdf.

Ho, A. S. P., Watkins, D., & Kelly, M. (2001). The conceptual change approach to improving teaching and learning: An evaluation of a Hong Kong staff development programme. *Higher Education, 42*(2), 143–169.

Hutchings, P., Huber, M. T., & Golde, C. M. (2006). *Integrating work and life: A vision for a changing academy.* Retrieved from http://www.carnegiefoundation .org/perspectives/sub.asp?key=245&subkey=2003.

Hutchings, P., & Shulman, L. S. (1999). The scholarship of teaching: New elaborations, new developments. *Change, 31*(5), 10–15.

Johnson, G. (2004). *Top 5: IBM.* Retrieved from http://www.trainingmag.com/msg/ search/article_display.jsp?vnu_econtent_id=1000442186.

Lewis, K. G. (1996). Faculty development in the United States: A brief history. *The International Journal for Academic Development, 2*(2), 26–33.

Massy, W. F., Wilger, A. K., & Colbeck, C. (1994). Departmental cultures and teaching quality: Overcoming "hollowed" collegiality. *Change, 26*(4), 11–20.

McNeil, D. (2008, July 11). *Facing enrollment crisis: Japanese universities fight to attract students* [Electronic version]. Retrieved from http://chronicle.com/weekly/ v54/i44/44a01701.htm?utm_source=pm&utm_medium=en.

Miller, R. (2001). *Use of part-time faculty in higher education/Numbers and impact: Briefing paper of the Greater Expectations National Panel.* Retrieved from http:// www.greaterexpectations.org/briefing_papers/parttimefaculty.html.

National Center for Educational Statistics (NCES). (2002). *Digest of educational statistics 2002.* Retrieved from http://nces.ed.gov/pubsearch/pubsinfo.asp?pubid =2003060.

National Center for Educational Statistics (NCES). (2007). *Digest of educational statistics 2007.* Retrieved from http://nces.ed.gov/programs/digest/d07/ch_1.asp.

National Center for Public Policy and Higher Education (NCPPHE). (2006). *Measuring up 2006: The national report card on education.* Retrieved from http://mea suringup.highereducation.org/_docs/2006/NationalReport_2006.pdf.

North, J., & Scholl, S. (1979). POD: The founding of a national network. *POD Quarterly, 1*(1).

Polich, S. (2008). Assessment of faculty learning community program: Do faculty members really change? In D. R. Robertson & L. B. Nilson (Eds.), *To improve the academy* (Vol. 27). San Francisco, CA: Jossey-Bass.

Postareff, L., Lindblom-Ylänne, S., & Nevgi, A. (2007). The effect of pedagogical training on teaching in higher education. *Teaching and Teacher Education, 23*(1), 557–571.

Prebble, T., Hargraves, H., Leach, L., Naidoo, K., Suddaby, G., & Zepke, N. (2005). *Impact of student support services and academic development programmes on student outcomes in undergraduate tertiary study: A synthesis of the research.* Retrieved from http://www.educationcounts.govt.nz/publications/tertiary_educa tion/5519.

Professional and Organizational Network in Higher Education (POD). (2002). *What is faculty development?* Retrieved from http://www.podnetwork.org/devel opment.htm/.

Rischard, J. F. (2002). *High noon: Twenty global issues, twenty years to solve them.* New York: Basic Books.

Rust, C. (1998). The impact of educational development workshops on teachers' practice. *The International Journal for Academic Development, 3*(1), 72–80.

Stes, A., Clement, M., & Van Petegem, P. (2007). The effectiveness of a faculty training program: Long term and institutional impact. *The International Journal for Academic Development, 12*(2), 99–109.

Sullivan, W. M., & Rosin, M. S. (2008). *A new agenda for education: Shaping a life of the mind for practice.* San Francisco, CA: Jossey-Bass.

The 2007–2008 Almanac: Trends in faculty employment. (2007). Retrieved from http://chronicle.com/weekly/almanac/2007/nation/0102503.htm.

PART ONE

FIVE CASE STUDIES AND A
COMPARATIVE ANALYSIS

I

FACULTY DEVELOPMENT IN CANADIAN UNIVERSITIES

K. Lynn Taylor and Denis Bédard

For almost 40 years, Canadian universities have invested in formal faculty development initiatives as a strategy to build teaching and learning capacity in our institutions (Wilcox, 1997). In keeping with the ethos of autonomy that characterizes our university system, the approaches to faculty development that have evolved over this time are quite diverse. They are shaped by the institutional cultures, faculty expertise, and resources of each academic community. Consequently, the Canadian experience offers not so much a so-called national model as a faculty development framework built on traditional academic values of inquiry, shared expertise, and collegial problem solving. This framework incorporates many different approaches to building more effective teaching and learning environments. The diversity of approaches illustrates rich opportunities for engaging colleagues from across disciplines—and institutions—in developing the practice and scholarship of teaching and learning. This chapter describes the history of faculty development practice in Canada and the current contextual factors contributing to the development of our field. We provide an overview of structures and programs across the country and discuss some of the challenges shaping the future of faculty development practice and scholarship. When pertinent, we highlight the distinctions characterizing the evolution of faculty development initiatives in Quebec's francophone universities, compared to those in the rest of Canada.

Conceptualizing Faculty Development

Faculty development and its related terms have carried different meanings over time and across countries. In North America, developers traditionally distinguished among *instructional, faculty,* and *organizational* development (Diamond, 2005). From the outset, Canadian developers distinguished between instructional development (which focused on the skills and knowledge necessary to plan effective instruction) and faculty development (which could include the development of "instructional materials, the physical plant, or the relative value placed on teaching by the institution" [Shore, 1974]). Most recently the development role has grown to often include organizational development related to building teaching and learning capacity at the institutional level. As development roles diversified, English Canadian developers adopted the term *educational developers* (Wilcox, 1997) to reflect their broader responsibilities, not only to individual teachers, but also to academic programs, the physical and technological learning environment, and administrative policies and practices that support effective learning and teaching experiences. In the new vernacular, educational development represents a synergy among instructional, faculty, and organizational development as we engage with colleagues in the development of individual teachers and courses, curriculum development at the program level (Cook, 2000), and problem solving and change at the institutional level (Diamond, 2005; Fletcher & Patrick, 1998; Hart, 1997; MacDonald, 2002).

In Quebec, francophone educational developers commonly refer to their role as *conseiller pédagogique.*[1] While their traditional focus was more on instructional and faculty development, the organizational development function is growing in importance. This shift was first manifested by allocating development resources to deal specifically with the integration of technology into teaching activities. More recently, targeted funding to support development focused on strategic objectives continues to mobilize development efforts at the system level at the Université du Québec. Although not used in direct translation, the term *educational developer* characterizes the work of the *conseiller pédagogique* in more pedagogically proactive universities such as the network of the Université du Québec and the Université de Sherbrooke.

Given the degree of autonomy within the Canadian postsecondary sector, it is not surprising that, while these major trends in the evolution of development roles are common to some degree across institutions, the specific organizational strategies for their implemention vary widely. The traditional development role was conceptualized as service to colleagues, so the role has a strong practice orientation. Within the field, the practice domains vary according to the priorities of the institutions and the expertise of individual developers. At many universities, the emphasis is on faculty and/or graduate student development. The trend toward organizational development is driven by the need to change institutional structures, policies and, more broadly, reward systems to support teaching development for these constituencies and the teaching mission. In others, a strategic priority to increase the use of technology in teaching has contributed to organizing instructional and faculty development resources to support this goal. In each case, the roles of individual developers may be specialized in a particular domain of practice, or they may cross faculty, organizational, or technology development, depending on the goals and resources of the academic community.

Although effective development practice depends on situating the development of teaching and learning in the context of a deep understanding of the nature of academic work and the culture of academic communities, the focus in Canada remains largely on the teaching and learning domain. In most universities, the scope of educational development is distinct from that of *academic development* as it is practiced in Australia and the UK. It is also distinct from *professional development* as it is practiced in parts of Europe (Rege Colet, chapter 2), where the development of the research role is commonly included (Brew & Boud, 1996). As the field matures in practice, and professionalization of the role evolves, the scholarship dimension of educational development also grows. Increasingly, educational developers pursue inquiry into their own practice and often, in collaboration with faculty colleagues, into aspects of teaching and learning. For example, the Université de Montréal gave its development center the additional mandate to engage in research activities, mostly characterized as action research projects. In a similar initiative, the University of British Columbia founded the Institute for the Scholarship of Teaching and Learning (http://www.tag.ubc.ca/about/institute/ISoTL.php) to foster research on student learning at the university. Such initiatives facilitate change in teaching and learning practice, but they also document the change processes and the impact of new practices on the teachers and students involved, thereby contributing to evidence-based practice and scholarship in the field.

For purposes of this chapter then, the term *educational development* refers to our complex and largely negotiated roles in facilitating the broad educational development needs of individuals, programs, and institutions.

The Political Context

To understand the evolution of educational development in Canada, one has to appreciate regulation of higher education in our country. According to the terms of the Canadian constitution, education falls under provincial and territorial jurisdiction. Because Canadian universities are publicly funded to a large extent, individual provinces and territories regulate and accredit university education, and there is no legislated mechanism for national coordination (Gregor, 1997).[2] Even though provincial governments do exercise more direct control through their funding authority, both the provincial and federal levels of government have supported a high level of autonomy in the university sector in the past.

In the absence of government infrastructure at the national level, a number of academic organizations have undertaken national advocacy and coordination roles with respect to the development of higher education, including the Society for Teaching and Learning in Higher Education (STLHE) (http://www.mcmaster.ca/stlhe/welcome.htm), the Association of Universities and Colleges of Canada (AUCC) (http://www.aucc.ca/index_e .html), the Canadian Society for the Study of Higher Education (CSSHE) (http://umanitoba.ca/outreach/csshe/), and the Canadian Association for University Teachers (CAUT) (http://www.caut.ca/).

Although there have been a number of valuable ad hoc initiatives within and between these academic organizations, their efforts have been fragmented. As a result, their well-intentioned plans and their interactions with federal and provincial governments have had limited strategic impact on enhancing teaching and learning across the Canadian university system.

However, with more than one million full- and part-time students, 34,000 full-time faculty, and 35% of the research and development activity in the country (Canadian Association of University Teachers [CAUT], 2007; Council of Ministers of Education, Canada [CMEC], 2005) invested in 120 public and not-for-profit, degree-granting institutions (CAUT, 2007), the need for more cooperation across jurisdictions is emerging. Pressing issues include meeting the learning needs of a larger and more diverse student population, improving the effectiveness of university teaching, responding to the training needs of the employment community (Altbach & Lewis, 1997; Canadian Council on Learning, 2006), enhancing mechanisms for research coordination, and streamlining the transferability of university credits and credentials (CMEC, 1998, 2005). While jurisdictional relationships are not likely to change, there are ongoing discussions across levels of government and with concerned academic institutions and associations about how to address some of these issues through policy initiatives rather than legislation (Christensen & Rog, 2006; CMEC, 2005).

In the context of these discussions, the political status quo in Canada began to change in the mid-1990s when some provincial governments started to play a more direct role in the affairs of universities. Indeed, the province of Quebec made university financing conditional on meeting specific performance goals having to do with, for example, the number of graduating students. All universities in the province had to agree with the government on specific performance goals, covering a five-year period, presented in the form of a *contrat de performance*. The political context for these universities had changed in that the notion of accountability of universities was set forth in explicit terms. The quality of teaching and its impact on students' performance and academic success was no longer just an internal issue or one having to do with concern for student learning or reputation. It now had direct impact on the financial health of the institution.

This trend continues. In a recent review of postsecondary education in Ontario, Bob Rae (2005) acknowledged the balance that needs to be struck between, on the one hand, "academic freedom" and "self-government and "institutional flexibility" (p. 16), and on the other, the responsibility of institutions to implement appropriate and transparent accountability and business practices. While cautioning against approaches to accountability that are "too heavy-handed or too intrusive" (p. 16) and "too expensive" (p. 17), Rae recommended establishment of

> a Council on Higher Education, reporting to the Minister of Training, Colleges and Universities, to: advise government on how to achieve its learning mission, set targets and measures for improvement, monitor and report on performance and outcomes, [and] coordinate research on higher education and encourage best practices. (p. 30)

As a consequence of Rae's report, the province of Ontario established an arm's-length agency, the Higher Education Quality Council of Ontario, which actively funds research and provides evidence-based policy advice to government to foster the improvement of postsecondary education quality, access, and accountability in Ontario (Higher Education Quality Council of Ontario [HEQCO], 2008).

Although government maintains respect for the work of universities, it is setting clear expectations for increased accountability in terms of the quality of students' learning experiences and for a strong return on investment in the university sector more generally. It is in this governance context that the faculty development practice in Canada has emerged and continues to develop.

The Academic Context

As the higher-education system is evolving, so too is the role of educational development. Although colleagues have always consulted each other on teaching issues, formal programs for educational development were established in the late 1960s, with the first educational development center founded in 1969 at McGill University in Montreal. Throughout the 1970s, educational development centers proliferated, particularly in Ontario, where, from 1973 to 1980, the Ontario Universities Program for Instructional Development (OUPID) received $2.5 million to fund individual and institutional educational development projects (Elrick, 1990). During the 1980s, there was a temporary period of retrenchment, when only two universities established educational development centers (University of Alberta and Dalhousie University). A number of developments contributed to the subsequent explosion in educational development units in the last 20 years.

One critical development was the emergence of a scholarly infrastructure to support development of teaching and learning in our institutions. The Canadian Society for the Study of Higher Education was founded in 1969, and the Professional Development Committee (later called the Teaching Effectiveness Committee) of the Canadian Association of University Teachers was also active during this period, advocating for the widespread use of teaching dossiers, among other measures. When OUPID was terminated in 1980, the Society for Teaching and Learning in Higher Education emerged as a national voice (particularly for English-speaking universities) advocating for the development and recognition of teaching in Canadian universities; it continues to sponsor a national annual conference on teaching and learning. French-speaking colleagues from Quebec, Belgium, Switzerland, and France founded the *Association internationale de pédagogie universitaire* (AIPU). This association has emerged as an influential force in the development of teaching and learning at francophone universities in Canada and in Europe.

Also during the 1970–1990 period, student ratings of instruction became widespread, with 94% of Canadian universities reporting their use (Donald & Saroyan, 1991). Although the perceived credibility of these measures varied across academic communities, their almost universal use raised awareness of teaching quality among a broad cross-section of the Canadian professoriate. The introduction of student ratings of instruction contributed directly to the development and widespread use of teaching dossiers (sometimes called portfolios) as faculty sought to diversify the perspectives from which their teaching was evaluated. The movement to evaluate teaching also created pressure for educational development resources to support faculty in responding to the feedback they received from students. More indirectly, the widespread use of teaching evaluation contributed to the development of dedicated programs to foster teaching effectiveness of graduate students and early-career faculty who now were expected to demonstrate teaching competence, as indicated by these instruments, from the outset of their career.

By the onset of the 1990s, the educational development function was poised to flourish. First, the AUCC-sponsored Commission of Inquiry on Canadian University Education engaged a broad range of stakeholders from across the country in discussions about the roles of universities in society. In his seminal report on these hearings, Stuart Smith strongly criticized the priority Canadian institutions gave to teaching, and identified the need for more resources to support the development of teaching and curriculum; even more radically, it called for a fundamental shift in how teaching was valued in most universities (Smith, 1991). Second, in 1998 the Council of Ministers of Education of Canada circulated a working paper that invited consultations on public expectations for postsecondary education (CMEC, 1998). The themes identified, which closely reflected the outcomes of the Smith inquiry report, included quality, accountability, accessibility, mobility, relevance and responsiveness, and research and scholarship. Considering the earlier trend stressing university performance, pressure for accountability—and change—was strong.

It is also in this context that the major French-speaking universities in Quebec established educational development centers in the 1990s. Laval University in Quebec City was among the first to do so in 1996, and the growth of centers continued through 2002 with the creation of a center at the Université du Québec à Montréal (UQAM). In addition to the trends operating in English Canada, two more factors contributed to the creation of these centers. The first was the need for Quebec universities to support the program evaluation process within their own walls. For example, the Université de Sherbrooke first instituted the *Bureau d'appui aux programmes* in 1993, before changing the statutes and mission of the office to those of an educational development center in 1997. Another influential factor was the implementation and fast-growing use of information and communication technology (ICT) within the universities throughout the 1980s and 1990s. Using ICT in the classroom offered an opportunity to emphasize teaching and learning and the development of pedagogical skills. Consequently, many educational development centers offer technological support to teachers as it relates to teaching and learning. In a different era, this fundamental shift in the responsiveness of universities to the expectations of students, governments, and the public at large may have been unthinkable, but times had changed.

In the current context, Canadian institutions are on the cusp of an unprecedented opportunity for change in educational development practice. Because of the age profile of our current professoriate and, to a lesser extent, because of increasing enrollments, the faculty cohort in our universities is undergoing massive renewal. In the decade leading up to 2010, it is expected that the Canadian faculty cohort will see a turnover of two-thirds of its members through retirement and will grow by an additional 10,000 in new positions (CMEC, 2005). This opportunity to meet the teaching development needs of new professors and influence policy changes to reflect the important role of teaching in most faculty careers is generating unprecedented growth in educational development. Given the strong spirit of autonomy and academic freedom that characterizes Canadian universities and the decentralized nature of their regulation, the structure and function of an expanding system of educational development units is taking many different forms.

Educational Development: Diversity of Function and Form

Educational development in Canadian universities is in great part a product of local values, needs, traditions, resources, and priorities. Consequently, it takes many forms. If one examines the diversity that can be observed from a developmental perspective, the patterns are more transparent. In the early years of educational development, the emphasis was on developing the fundamental teaching skills of individual faculty colleagues (Donald, 1986). Gradually, academia came to understand the development of teaching and learning capacity in multifaceted and more complex ways. In addition to assisting colleagues in developing teaching competence, the expertise of educational developers was called on to help institutions in developing methods of assessing teaching performance, adjusting reward systems to raise the profile of teaching in academic careers, and changing administrative practices to foster the development of productive learning environments (Harrison, 2002). More recently, educational developers are providing growing support for discipline-based inquiry into teaching and learning by collaborating with colleagues to facilitate the scholarship of teaching and learning, and by advocating for recognition of this work in faculty career progression (Bass, 1999; McKinney, 2004). In all of these endeavors, educational developers may be called on to advise, educate, or facilitate change (Wright, 1995).

Harrison (2002) gives a brief overview of how these different levels of involvement can translate into a range of educational development programs in different academic communities. One dimension of educational development programs is: "Who participates?" Some programs focus on new faculty or graduate students and may include undergraduate students employed as teaching assistants. Increasingly, participation in educational development programs extends across the career span as colleagues seek advice on refining their teaching, responding to new teaching situations, or designing scholarship of teaching and learning projects. In addition to individual colleagues, educational developers may collaborate with entire academic units on a particular teaching issue, such as evaluation of student learning, or on larger curriculum development projects, such as implementation of problem-based learning (PBL) or integration of service learning. With growing frequency, developers work at the institutional level to contribute to policy and practice development that fosters a positive teaching and learning environment or to institutional problem solving on issues such as increasing retention rates or fostering academic integrity.

Another facet of "Who participates?" is the educational developers themselves. There are few national or international opportunities to prepare for careers in educational development. In the field's early days, colleagues with reputations for outstanding teaching were recruited to support the development of other colleagues, as were colleagues who held academic credentials in associated fields such as education or the learning sciences. Many of these early positions were part-time or term limited. As recognition for educational development as a field of practice and scholarship grows, persons with particular expertise and/or longer-term commitment to educational development are staffing these positions permanently. At the same time, the field recognizes the value of faculty colleagues' teaching and learning expertise, and educational development units are increasingly integrating a faculty associate or teaching scholar/chair position in their staffing plans. These positions are ideally situated to increase the flow of teaching and learning knowledge across disciplines and between academic units and educational development centers.

A second dimension of educational development programs is: "How do we engage in the development process across these multiple tasks and constituencies?" Opportunities to participate in structured degree programs in higher education such as those at the University of Calgary are rare. However, there is growth in more formal, non-degree programs for graduate students and new faculty. Now more than 25 institutions offer a credit course in teaching and learning or a recognized certificate in teaching and learning to graduate students. Participation in these programs is mostly voluntary, though some academic programs have made such programs a requirement of their degree, such as the doctoral program in management offered jointly by Montreal's four universities: McGill, Université de Montréal, Concordia, and Université du Québec à Montréal. Formal programs for new faculty are less common. A notable exception is the École Polytechnique de Montréal (Université de Montréal), where, since the early 1990s, all newly hired professors must agree to mandatory training on teaching and learning supervised by the pedagogical advisors of the educational development center. More recently, recognized credentialing of new academic staff through comprehensive development programs (albeit based on voluntary participation) is emerging in well-recognized institutions, including Queen's University, the University of British Columbia, and Ryerson University.

Participation in educational development is on a voluntary basis and informal. Depending on the circumstances, the most appropriate development strategies might include more direct teaching roles, such as individual consultations; provision of resource materials; workshops on fundamental teaching strategies; or orientation of new academic staff. In less well-defined situations, mentoring and peer consultation, shared problem solving, or facilitating a "learning community" (Cox, 2004) to explore or resolve an issue may be more appropriate. The scope of these activities demands expertise about one's academic community, academic culture, and teaching and learning and the processes of facilitating learning under a range of conditions (Taylor, 2005a).

A third dimension of educational development is: "What is its organizational structure?" This dimension also varies across institutional contexts. How educational development units are situated in the organizational architecture of each university is largely the result of the individual institutions' culture and established infrastructure. The most common arrangement is that educational development resources are housed in a freestanding central unit that reports directly to the vice president–academic or the associate vice president–academic (or equivalent position). Most of the practice community sees this combination of organizational autonomy and direct reporting lines to the senior administrators of the university as the most desirable organizational structure. Examples include Dalhousie University (http://www.learningandteaching.dal.ca), Université de Sherbrooke, and Université de Montréal. In smaller institutions, it is not unusual to have educational development initiatives led through a committee of faculty colleagues (for example, St. Francis Xavier University) whose members voluntarily coordinate educational development opportunities for colleagues. Other organizational structures include locating the educational development function within a related unit (for example, The Centre for Higher Education Research and Development at the University of Manitoba or within Continuing Education at Memorial University of Newfoundland). There are also faculty-based educational development units, an organizational model that is well established in medicine and is a growing trend in dentistry and engineering.

At the opposite end of the discipline-specific/general spectrum, the emergence of the concept *learning commons* places educational development in the context of an integrated array of resources for student and faculty learning, such as at the University of Saskatchewan (http://www.usask.ca/ulc/). Such commons offer student support in such areas as study skills, writing development, and information literacy, and resources to faculty in areas including technology and pedagogy. Most recently, the emergence of institutes for the scholarship of teaching and learning, such as at the University of British Columbia and the University of Toronto, provides yet another organizational structure to support the building of teaching and learning capacity, often in conjunction with more traditional educational development resources. Whatever the organizational structure, it is critical that educational development units work in partnership with faculty colleagues and other resource providers, such as libraries and academic computing, and that expertise is applied in the discipline and personal context that characterizes each case.

In Canada, interactions among participants, strategies for engagement, and institutional context result in a diverse mix of educational development services and strategies. The complexity of the educational development task and the range of choices to be made may be best illustrated with an example from the Center for Learning and Teaching at Dalhousie University.

Figure 1.1 represents an overview of the work of a particular educational development center, which serves three primary constituencies (graduate students, new faculty, and general faculty) in three domains (teaching development, curriculum development, and career development). This center also collaborates with academic departments and with the institution as a whole to develop programs, practices, and policies that enhance teaching and learning experiences. At the heart of this model are the needs of the constituencies served and the research base that informs all aspects of engagement in the academic community. While the specific strategies for engagement (the outer ring) will vary over time and across tasks, the orientation to client needs and evidence-based practice are stable components.

At present, the specific activities of this center engage different constituencies and goals. Resources for graduate student development include a nested program of individual consultation, an orientation for teaching assistants, a monthly professional development series for graduate students, an academically recognized course on teaching and learning, and a comprehensive Certificate in University Teaching. For new academic staff, there is an orientation program, a series of professional development opportunities focused mainly on teaching and learning, and an integrated program founded on a week long course development workshop as well as follow-up activities as each cohort of participants implements its planned courses. For everyone involved in teaching, there are regular opportunities to participate

FIGURE 1.1
An Example of Educational Practice in Canada Center

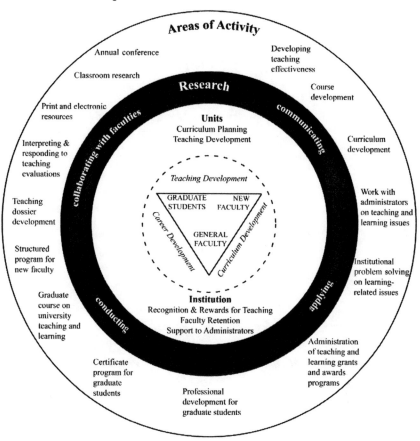

in workshops, discussion groups on specific themes, peer consultation, individual consultations, and access to print and electronic teaching and learning resources. The scholarship of teaching and learning is fostered through two modest grants programs and an annual teaching and learning conference. Departments may request custom workshops and other more sustained types of collaboration with respect to specific issues (for example, critical thinking integration in a specific discipline), as may institutions as a whole (for example, academic integrity). Also at the institutional level, staff from this center participate widely in the committee infrastructure of the university to advocate for and influence decision making that has an impact on teaching and learning, to coordinate a number of teaching award programs, and to raise awareness of the teaching and learning mission of the university through creating and contributing to institutional communications on the topic. In other universities, specific activities and services include combinations of these and other strategies, depending on the needs, resources, and culture of the institution.

Some aspects of this illustrative case reflect the slow but systematic shifts in educational development practice from more individually based practices to more program-based interventions. Three trends explain this situation. First, the rate and pace at which new or innovative programs are being implemented has broadened the scope of educational development to include more curriculum work at the program level. At the Université de Sherbrooke or at the Université de Montréal, for example, a substantial number of programs have implemented major pedagogical innovations, such as the use of PBL across the curriculum, particularly in professional fields such as medicine or engineering and in the human sciences (Bédard, Louis, Bélisle, & Viau, 2007). Second, participants in educational development programs increasingly value the formal credentialing and recognition of their investments in teaching development. In particular, certificates are offered to graduate students and new faculty. Third, educational development units themselves value the higher visibility and impact potential offered through program-level work.

This shift has resulted in a reallocation of educational development staff resources. In return for getting involved at a program level, developers engage a larger number of faculty members in meaningful and sustained ways, and their work becomes more visible to administrators. Because financing and allocation of resources are always key issues, these initiatives demonstrate the value of their involvement, not only in preparing academic staff to teach more effectively, but also in meeting the institution's pedagogical and organizational needs.

This shift is also related to development and implementation of the scholarship of teaching. Indeed, the work of educational developers is increasingly discipline-based and actively promotes the idea of inquiry into teaching and learning. In effect, they become brokers of pedagogical expertise who are able to guide, support, and connect colleagues in accessing the appropriate resources and collaborators to plan, implement, and publish studies demonstrating the impact of specific teaching and learning strategies or program development in diverse discipline contexts.

Challenges and Future Directions

As a community of practice, Canadian educational developers face multiple and sometimes competing demands. From our largely centralized locations, we must provide support for teaching and learning development that is contextualized in the experiences of individual colleagues, in the disciplines, and in particular institutional cultures. Increasingly, we are expected to contribute to building institutional teaching and learning capacity by aligning our development efforts with institutional goals, priorities, and rewards while still maintaining the integrity of our own practice and respecting the academic freedom and confidentiality of the individual colleagues with whom we work. The emergence of the scholarship of teaching and learning further challenges us to lend our expertise as researchers to the development process. In all of these endeavors, we strive to remain grounded in the ethical principles that guide our practice (Knight & Wilcox, 1998).

One of these ethical principles is a commitment to learning in our own field. The decentralized nature of the Canadian university system has encouraged multiple models and approaches to educational development from which we have all learned. One of the most important contexts in which we share learning about educational development (especially in English Canada) is through the Educational Developers Caucus of the Society for Teaching and Learning in Higher Education (STLHE) (http://www .mcmaster.ca/stlhe/subgroups/edcaucus.htm). Through meetings, conferences, a Web page, and an active listserv, colleagues share the practices and scholarship that contribute to the development of our field. Regionally, developers benefit from organized networks such as in the Atlantic region (http://www.atlanticuniversities.ca/aau_2116.html) and in Quebec (*le réseau Belgique–Suisse–Québec* [BSQ]). These professional learning opportunities are essential since educational development specialists have few opportunities for formal training in their diverse roles. One notable exception is the Mobility Project (Frenay & Saroyan, chapter 6), which resulted in the design of a structured academic program to prepare participants from four different countries for educational/faculty development roles.

In a recent planning process, Canadian educational developers identified learning needs that reflect the emerging trends in our field (Taylor, 2005b). An overriding trend is the unprecedented growth in the educational development function. As in other countries, our institutions are seeing increasing expectations for accountability in the face of larger, more diverse student populations; mandated curriculum goals; and decreasing resources. As universities and colleges recognize the value of educational development expertise in the development of individuals, programs, and institutions, the number of new colleagues involved in the field and the diversity of our work increases. In just the last several years, membership in the Educational Developers Caucus alone has doubled, and professional development opportunities for less-experienced developers are a strongly expressed need in our community. At least two new initiatives have been undertaken to address the critical need for both recruitment and professional development. Canadian developers are leading an international project, titled "Pathways to the Profession," in which they are documenting multiple pathways into the profession to encourage a diverse range of colleagues' entry into the educational development community (McDonald & Stockley, 2008). In a second project focusing on the professional development of practicing educational developers, Dawson and Britnell (2008) are engaging the educational development community in identifying specific educational development competencies required at three common stages in the career span: entry into the profession, experienced developer, and director of an educational development unit. These initiatives are well placed to inform the burgeoning professional development needs of the field.

A second trend is that our work in discipline contexts is growing, as both developers and discipline-based colleagues recognize the effectiveness of addressing specific learning issues in context. In turn, developers are seeking to learn more about disciplinary cultures and practices.

Third, for some time our work has been expanding in its focus to include curriculum development at the program level and change related to teaching and learning at the institutional level. This trend is reflected in requests for professional development in leadership, facilitating organizational change, and designing development programs for other academic administrators.

Fourth, the scholarship of teaching and learning has captured the imaginations of a broad cross-section of Canadian academics:

> A scholarship of teaching is not synonymous with excellent teaching. It requires a kind of "going meta," in which faculty frame and systematically investigate questions related to student learning—the conditions under which it occurs, what it looks like, how to deepen it, and so on—and to do so with an eye not only to improving their own classroom, but to advancing practice beyond it. (Hutchings & Shulman, 1999, p. 13)

In this work, educational developers often consult and/or collaborate more extensively in the design, implementation, interpretation, and communication of these scholarly initiatives, and they have made their own professional development in this area a priority.

Finally, educational developers in Canada are seeking to develop methods to demonstrate the effectiveness of their own practice. This task is especially challenging since the nature of much of the work is indirect. We are in the business of helping individuals, programs, and institutions enhance the impact of student learning experiences, and it is an ongoing task to find measures that reflect the influence of our work in the dynamic synergy of teaching and learning.

Educational development in Canada has come of age. It is maturing as a robust and responsive field of practice and scholarship and is gaining credibility in a diverse range of institutions. In the dynamic environment of contemporary universities and colleges, it will continue to develop as it engages and fosters change in our postsecondary learning environments and continues to benefit from the experience and knowledge of national and international colleagues.

Notes

1. The term *agent de développement pédagogique* is also used at the Université de Montréal.

2. The federal government retains direct responsibility for postsecondary education of aboriginal peoples, military personnel, and persons in federal correctional institutions only. Indirectly it funds postsecondary education through transfer payments to the provinces, a national student loan program, and a registered educational savings plan CMEC, 2005). However, these contributions result in little direct federal control.

References

Altbach, P. G., & Lewis, L. S. (1997). Professorial attitudes: An international survey. In P. G. Altbach & M. J. Finkelstein (Eds.), *Contemporary higher education: The academic profession* (pp. 87–93). New York: Garland.

Bass, R. (1999). The scholarship of teaching: What's the problem? *Inventio: Creative Thinking About Learning and Teaching, 1*(1), 1–10.

Bédard, D., Louis, R., Bélisle, M., & Viau, R. (2007). Problem and project based learning in engineering at the University of Sherbrooke: Impacts on students' and teachers' perceptions. In E. De Graaff & A. Kolmos (Eds.), *Management of change: Implementation of problem-based and project-based learning in engineering* (pp. 109–128). Rotterdam, The Netherlands: Sense.

Brew, A., & Boud, D. (1996). Preparing for new academic roles: An holistic approach to development. *The International Journal for Academic Development, 1*(2), 17–25.

Canadian Association of University Teachers (CAUT). (2007). *CAUT almanac of post-secondary education in Canada.* Ottawa, Canada: Author.

Canadian Council on Learning. (2006). *Canadian post-secondary education: A positive record, an uncertain future.* Retrieved from http://www.ccl-cca.ca/CCL/Reports/PostSecondaryEducation?Language=EN.

Christensen, H. J., & Rog, E. (2006). *Roundtable on research, teaching and learning.* Guelph, Canada: University of Guelph.

Cook, C. E. (2000). The role of a teaching centre in curricular reform. In D. Lieberman & C. M. Wehlburg (Eds.), *To improve the academy* (Vol. 19, pp. 217–231). Bolton, MA: Anker.

Council of Ministers of Education, Canada (CMEC) (1998). *Public expectations of postsecondary education in Canada.* Retrieved from http://www.cmec.ca/post sec/pseexpect.en.stm.

Council of Ministers of Education, Canada (CMEC) (2005). *Education in Canada.* Retrieved from http://www.cmec.ca/index.en.html.

Cox, M. D. (2004). Introduction to faculty learning communities. In M. D. Cox & L. Richlin (Eds.), *New directions for teaching and learning: Vol. 97. Building faculty learning communities* (pp. 5–24). San Francisco, CA: Jossey-Bass.

Dawson, D., & Britnell, J. (2008, February). *Spanning the career of an educational developer one competency at a time.* Paper presented at the Educational Developers' Caucus Conference, Vancouver, Canada.

Diamond, R. M. (2005). The institutional change agency: The expanding role of academic support centers. In S. Chadwick-Blossey & D. R. Robertson (Eds.), *To improve the academy* (Vol. 23, pp. 24–37). Bolton, MA: Anker.

Donald, J. G. (1986). Teaching and learning in higher education in Canada: Changes over the last decade. *The Canadian Journal of Higher Education, 16*(3), 77–84.

Donald, J. G., & Saroyan, A. (1991). *Assessing the quality of teaching in Canadian universities.* Ottawa, Canada: Association of Universities and Colleges of Canada, Commission of Inquiry on Canadian University Education.

Elrick, M. (1990). Improving instruction in universities: A case study of the Ontario universities program for instructional development (OUPID). *The Canadian Journal of Higher Education, 20*(2), 61–79.

Fletcher, J. J., & Patrick, S. K. (1998). Not just workshops anymore: The role of academic development in reframing academic priorities. *The International Journal for Academic Development, 3*(1), 39–46.

Gregor, A. (1997). The universities of Canada. In *Commonwealth universities yearbook 1997–1998* (Vol. 1, pp. 315–341). London: Association of Commonwealth Universities.

Harrison, J. E. (2002). *The quality of university teaching: Faculty performance and accountability. A literature review (N° CSSHE-PF-21).* Winnipeg, Canada: Canadian Society for the Study of Higher Education.

Hart, G. (1997). Modelling a learning environment: Towards a learning organization. *The International Journal for Academic Development, 2*(2), 50–55.

Higher Education Quality Council of Ontario (HEQCO) (2008). *About us.* Retrieved from http://www.heqco.ca/inside.php?&ID=1.

Hutchings, P., & Shulman, L. S. (1999). The scholarship of teaching: New elaborations, new developments. *Change, 31*(5), 10–15.

Knight, P. T., & Wilcox, S. (1998). Effectiveness and ethics in educational development: Changing contexts, changing notions. *The International Journal for Academic Development, 3,* 97–106.

MacDonald, R. (2002). Academic development: Research, evaluation and changing practice in higher education. In R. MacDonald & J. Wisdom (Eds.), *Academic and educational development: Research, evaluation and changing practice in higher education* (pp. 3–13). London: Falmer.

McDonald, J., & Stockley, D. (2008). Pathways to the profession of educational development: An international perspective. *The International Journal for Academic Development, 13*(3), 213–218.

McKinney, K. (2004). The scholarship of teaching and learning: Past lessons, current challenges, and future visions. In C. Wehlburg & S. Chadwick-Blossey (Eds.), *To improve the academy* (Vol. 22, pp. 3–19). Bolton, MA: Anker.

Rae, B. (2005). *Ontario: A leader in learning. Report and recommendations.* Retrieved from www.uwo.ca/pvp/president_reports/documents/RaeFinalReport.pdf.

Shore, B. M. (1974). Instructional development in Canadian higher education. *The Canadian Journal of Higher Education, 4*(2), 45–53.

Smith, S. (1991). *Report of the commission of inquiry of Canadian university education.* Ottawa, Canada: Association of Universities and Colleges of Canada.

Taylor, K. L. (2005a). Academic development as institutional leadership: An interplay of person, role, strategy and institution. *The International Journal for Academic Development, 10*(1), 31–46.

Taylor, K. L. (2005b). *Proposal for a professional development plan for the educational developers' caucus.* Charlottetown, PEI, Canada: Educational Developers Caucus, Society for Teaching and Learning in Higher Education.

Wilcox, S. (1997). *Educational development in higher education.* Unpublished doctoral thesis, Ontario Institute for Studies in Education, University of Toronto, Canada.

Wright, W. A. (Ed.). (1995). *Teaching improvement practices: Successful strategies for higher education.* Bolton, MA: Anker.

2

FACULTY DEVELOPMENT IN SWITZERLAND

A Study of French-Speaking Universities

Nicole Rege Colet

F aculty development is not high on the agenda of Swiss universities, and institutional policy pays little attention to promoting academic development. It is surprising, however, that many higher-education institutions have invested in faculty development centers since the late 1990s. For this reason, the lack of policy may seem a paradox. This chapter examines how the political context and the fight for autonomy led Swiss universities to develop support centers for teaching. It outlines the circumstances that supported the growth of the centers and tackles the question of defining faculty development in a multicultural and multilinguistic environment. It describes the functions of the centers in terms of their differences in missions and institutional settings and examines faculty training programs through the frameworks and teaching models supported by faculty developers in these centers. Finally, it highlights the strong potential for faculty development in higher-education institutions in Switzerland and argues that enhancing teaching and learning capacity within higher education depends on building up the community of faculty developers and recognizing the value of their expertise in educational development.

The Political Context: A New Form of Higher Education

Switzerland does not have a national higher-education system; each of the 26 cantons of the confederation is autonomously in charge of education. As of 2000, higher education has become a dual system comprising 10 cantonal universities and two federal institutes of technology as well as seven newly founded universities of applied sciences. The system is administered through a federal framework, and several bodies are involved in promoting higher-education policy and coordination (State Secretariat for Education and Research, 2005). The most important for research-based universities are the *Conférence universitaire suisse* (CUS) (Swiss University Conference) and the *Conférence des recteurs des universités suisses* (CRUS) (Rectors' Conference of the Swiss Universities). CUS brings together the directors of education from the cantons in charge of universities and representatives of the federal administration. Its main function is to set up efficient cooperation between the cantons and higher-education institutions. CRUS is a consultative body of university leaders and a private association that takes on mandates dealing with the implementation of reforms and issues such as curriculum, syllabus, and uniformity in conditions of admission to studies.

Until recently the higher-education system was described as heterogeneous. Differences between research-led institutions and professional institutions were often given as an explanation, but this also promoted a strong division between the two types of higher-education institutions. Governing of science and research by the Department of the Interior (Home Office) and professional training by the Department of Public Economy largely reinforced this division. However, the situation has been changing, beginning with the founding of universities of applied sciences in 2000. Casting these newly founded universities as counterparts or competitors to research-led institutions has helped build the tertiary education system as a whole.

Implementation of the Bologna Declaration has also strongly influenced the shaping of a new form of higher education (Rege Colet & Durand, 2004). In signing the declaration, CUS was able to justify unifying the system and challenged CRUS to apply the principles on a national scale. CRUS was asked by CUS to draft national guidelines to give higher education a common framework. The guidelines were adopted in December 2003 and are now being used in universities for curriculum development (*Conférence universitaire suisse occidentale* [CUSO], 2003).

In most cases, curriculum development has led to a stronger concern with pedagogical issues. For instance, the widespread use of the European Credit Transfer and Accumulation System (ECTS) has shed new light on defining learning outcomes and reconsidering student assessment. Facilitating access to university studies has become a priority for many institutions. Conditions (including acknowledgment of prior learning) for admission to master programs are being reviewed to attract new publics. Debate continues over the need to set out the qualifications framework following the Bergen ministerial meeting in May 2005 (Ministry of Education and Research of Norway, 2005). Finally, quality assurance related to teaching and learning in universities and, in particular, the measurement standards, are the source of animated discussion among representatives of the universities and the *Organe d'accréditation et d'assurance qualité* (OAQ) (Centre of Accreditation and Quality Assurance).

The Academic Context: Fostering Awareness in Teaching and Learning

The new form of higher education has forced universities to rethink their identity. Until the birth of universities of applied science, these institutions had no need to attract students and little urge to seek research funds. This competition-free environment no longer exists, and universities now have to contend with their new counterparts. This rivalry has encouraged universities to make bold statements about the pedagogical model that is the focus of their research-based teaching. The claims are daring, since a satisfactory definition of research-based teaching and how it is carried out in the classroom has yet to be given. However, the model holds weight in research-led institutions. The University of Geneva, for instance, cites its membership in the League of European Research Universities (LERU) and its participation in a survey by the University of Leuven on the links between research and teaching in teaching practices (Elen, 2005). There have been few substantive initiatives, however, and much remains to do done to arrive at a definitive model for university teaching and learning.

Higher-education teachers in Switzerland, as in many other countries, do not have to go through a formal training program to teach, which public authorities are now questioning. Because universities benefit from public funding, they are under increasing pressure for greater accountability of research and teaching activities. Internal and external quality assurance procedures have become a necessary trade-off to retain autonomy. For these reasons, evaluation of teaching effectiveness has become a priority for most universities and was the main motive for creating a faculty development center. This was reinforced in 2003 when OAQ was mandated to evaluate the internal quality assurance procedures of all Swiss universities (OAQ, 2005). Among the standards for measuring commitment to quality was the requirement that an institution have an organized unit in charge of evaluation. Other important criteria were training programs for teaching staff and a comprehensive system of teaching evaluation involving students.

Well before this formal evaluation for quality assurance, the link between student rating of courses and faculty training was acknowledged. Most training programs had started at about the same time in the 1990s, when evaluation of teaching effectiveness was introduced. However, attendance at programs has remained voluntary, albeit highly recommended. No university has yet taken steps to make training compulsory for new staff or teachers with poorly rated courses.

Strong emphasis is placed on research activities, and measurement of academic performance is based on research results and publications. Nevertheless, most institutions are developing policies on teaching activities for appointments and renewal of positions. For instance, while professorial appointments are still based on research achievements, candidates must now provide a sample lesson as evidence of their teaching skills. Unfortunately, and to the admission of hiring committees, the quality of these lessons bears little weight on final employment decisions. The University of Lausanne and the Institute of Technology of Lausanne have recently introduced the requirement of a teaching portfolio, including a report on student ratings, for appointment and renewal applications. Ongoing debate attests to the recognition of a split between teaching and research missions and the increasing complexity of both. There is considerable discussion in support of bringing together teaching and research missions, and some have suggested using performance indicators related to teaching activities. Recommendations are published regularly to bring them together, but very few substantive follow-up actions have been taken.

The issue of training future researchers has generated a new concern for teaching skills. To compete in an increasingly demanding international market, doctoral students must be thoroughly trained, not only in their discipline, but also in managing research and teaching. New doctoral programs, therefore, offer opportunities to train in fields such as teaching management, learning processes, instructional design, and e-learning.

Defining Faculty Development in the Social Context

Cultural and language differences in Switzerland make it difficult to discuss national models of teaching and draw up a comprehensive review of faculty development strategies. After a brief outline of the linguistic difficulties in simply translating *faculty development*, this chapter expands on the work carried out in French-language universities. There are three reasons for this focus on a regional linguistic group of institutions. The first is that the universities of applied science have just started their faculty development centers and use resources available in universities for implementing training programs. The second is that the centers of French-language universities have been working in a formal network for several years and have developed a model for faculty development. The third is complications arising from linguistic differences. For example, including German-language universities (which are also investing in faculty development) would entail a lengthy comparative work and distract from the main purpose of this chapter, which is to explain faculty development and its practice.

There is no straightforward translation available in French for the term *faculty development*. As English is the crossover language of the linguistic regions, the term *faculty development* is often used and even appears in the name of the national Swiss Faculty Development Network (SFDN). The French-language community must contend with the term *pédagogie universitaire*, which pertains to university teaching, but excludes activities more in keeping with professional or academic development (Knight, 2002; Knight & Trowler, 2001; Trigwell, 2003). Debate continues over whether *pédagogie universitaire* is a specific field of research or simply a set of actions to enhance teaching skills. A recent survey (Rege Colet, 2008) shows that the academic departments of universities do little research on higher education, whereas institutional research and support centers based in every university have been producing promising research results.

Faculty development activities in the German-language community come under the term *Hochschuldidaktik*, or didactics in higher education. Here again, semantics might imply a focus on instructional design or teaching skills. The term *didactics* also implies that there is an art of teaching—which can be taught—and that specific efforts have to be invested to make highly complex scientific knowledge accessible to all learners. Like their French-language colleagues, faculty developers in *Hochschuldidaktik* centers argue that their activities go beyond simply implementing faculty training programs.

For lack of suitable alternatives, both French- and German-language communities have accepted the English term *faculty development* to define their field of work. For a start, *faculty development* covers the wide range of educational activities carried out; as a generic term, it encompasses a host of educational issues. There are some other common terms: instructional development, for example, describes teaching practice, basic teaching skills, and course designing. Within the context of the Bologna process, curriculum development refers to changes and innovations in programs. Educational development is seen from a broader perspective than instructional design, with an emphasis on building teaching and learning capacity and supporting educational innovation and changes in teaching and learning models. Finally, professional development acknowledges the need to professionalize academic work and offer suitable training to satisfy research and teaching mandates. Because the term *faculty development* is an inclusive notion that is perceived as too broad for putting together a common framework, most centers would agree that educational development as defined above is a good description of their mission.

Role and Functions of Faculty Development Centers

As of 2005, all five institutions[1] of the French-language region of Switzerland had a faculty development unit. The first to establish a nonacademic structure was the Federal Institute of Technology, Lausanne[2], which started offering workshops and courses on pedagogical issues in the mid-1980s. The universities of Geneva and Lausanne followed in the late 1990s and immediately founded a regional network[3] (Réseau CFE, 2005) with the Institute of Technology to share expertise and develop a joint program in faculty development, a network open to all institutions of the region. The bilingual University of Fribourg has developed its own center with its longtime German-language partner, University of Bern. University of Neuchâtel took the step of creating its own center in 2005 and immediately applied for membership within the Réseau CFE.

All university centers are nonacademic centralized structures independent of departments and linked directly to the rector's office. Personnel consist of nonacademic staff with high academic qualifications in higher education or related fields. Only the University of Fribourg and the Institute of Technology have appointed a professor as head of their respective centers. The mandates of the centers vary from serving as an office of educational policy that implements institutional strategies in higher education or internal quality assurance procedures to serving as a unit of educational development that focuses on the quality of teaching and learning. Although their chief mission is to provide services for the academic community, the centers also conduct research on higher education. A stronger link between centers and academic units would enable joint research projects.

All university centers are engaged in promoting teaching and learning. They are required to provide training programs for teaching staff, to develop internal procedures for evaluation of teaching effectiveness, and to encourage pedagogical innovation. Activities are strongly influenced by the belief that educational quality will improve through a conceptual shift from a teacher-centered model of knowledge dissemination to a student-centered model of learning with an understanding of the process (Biggs, 1999; Kember & Kwan, 2002; Prosser & Trigwell, 1999). The Réseau CFE has drafted a framework paper on the faculty development model shared by its member universities (Rege Colet, Ricci, Paulino, & Berthiaume, 2006) that strongly emphasizes tailoring programs and consultation to meet teachers' needs. Dogmatic or prescriptive views on teaching have no place in these discussions. The network's commitment to the scholarship of teaching and learning through evidence-based knowledge as well as experiential knowledge acquired by teachers is spelled out, as are principles for organizing teacher training programs and defining learning outcomes. Finally, the network acknowledges the importance of internal and external evaluation of activities to achieve objectives and monitor educational development.

Activities, in keeping with what is traditionally proposed in educational development centers (Kreber, 1997; Weimer, 1990; Wright, 1995), include workshops, individual or departmental counseling, and evaluation centering on four domains. The first and perhaps most important domain involves training activities, including workshops, modules, and comprehensive programs on teaching and learning. The second domain deals with the use of information and communication technology (ICT), better known now as e-learning. The 1999 federal program, Swiss Virtual Campus (SVC), placed an emphasis on ICT as a mean of enhancing university teaching (SVC, 2005) and provided special funds for each university to build a support center. But rather than create a specialized unit that could not outlast the funding period, the French-language universities allocated funds to existing faculty development centers. The third domain tackles innovation in teaching and learning practices with a focus on problem-based teaching, student-centered learning, and self-directed studies. Developments of this type are limited to professional fields of study such as medicine and engineering. The last domain concerns evaluation of the quality of teaching and involves monitoring student evaluation of teaching activities, completing program or institutional evaluation, devising procedures for measuring innovative practice, and taking part in various forms of quality assurance procedures that relate to teaching.

Faculty development centers are constantly revising their agendas and renewing their actions according to institutional priorities. But, as stated above, they are also producing interesting research results in various domains of higher education and providing evidence-based knowledge on institutional change and teaching practice. As a result, both the activities and the studies of the centers have contributed to promoting a new profession and career possibilities in higher education.

Table 2.1 provides a summary of the missions and activities of the five centers and highlights their differences in institutional position, institutional mission, and areas of activities. Research mentioned as a mission means that an academic manages the center and can apply for research funds. Development options summarize how faculty developers see themselves as operating.

Teacher Training Programs and Activities

Since 2000, the Réseau CFE has hosted an annual program of 20 half- or full-day workshops that all teaching staff of the partner universities can attend free of charge. Program leaders often opt for half-day workshops, which seem to suit academic schedules—time being a critical factor in attendance at a non-compulsory workshop. Most teachers take part in at least two workshops per year, and every year a group of faithful supporters attends the entire program. Participants receive a certificate, and those who complete the program obtain additional certification. Content focuses chiefly on instructional design and deals with issues such as communication skills, teaching methods, and student assessment. Participants have the opportunity to experience interactive teaching methods that they can reproduce in their classroom. Some might argue that the workshops present only a series of tips

TABLE 2.1
Educational Development Units

	Position	Mission	Development Options	Activities
Institute of Technology, Lausanne	• Research in higher education • Educational development	• Services • Research	• Instructional • Educational • Academic	• Training programs • E-learning • Evaluation
University of Fribourg	• Research in higher education • Educational development	• Services • Research	• Instructional • Educational • Professional	• Training programs • E-learning
University of Geneva	• Educational development • Educational policy	• Services	• Instructional • Educational • Curriculum • Professional	• Training programs • E-learning • Innovative teaching and learning • Evaluation • Quality assurance
University of Lausanne	• Educational development	• Services	• Instructional • Educational	• Training programs • E-learning • Innovative teaching and learning • Evaluation • Quality assurance
University of Neuchâtel	• Educational development	• Services	• Instructional • Educational	• Training programs • Evaluation

and tricks for good teaching practice. However, the substantive underlying conceptual framework of the program is rooted in the conviction that teachers should have the best possible grasp of the learning process and constructive alignment (Biggs, 2002). Experience has shown that teachers are not open to conceptual reflection and are more concerned about coping with everyday reality. The advantage of building up pedagogical awareness as opposed to classroom management remains an open question.

The workshops develop the broad principles and trends in university teaching, but they cannot deal with specific teaching or learning issues. Therefore participants are encouraged to contact their institutions' faculty developers for individual guidance on their teaching practice. Many teachers have taken advantage of this opportunity and regularly consult their center. As a result, the workshops have become a good platform for promoting other forms of support for educational development.

Participation in teacher training programs is still voluntary, albeit encouraged and recommended. Since no institution has put forward a system to encourage or enforce professional development, attendance is very low. An analysis of participation rates shows that only 4% of teaching staff enroll in the Réseau CFE program (Durand, 2005). Two-thirds of the participants are women, who comprise only one-third of the teaching staff. Academics teaching in social sciences, where teaching loads are highest, are the most regular participants. Beginners routinely follow the program, while tenured professors attend only an occasional workshop.

At the start of the Réseau CFE program, all types of academic staff were targeted for workshops. However, the program leaders quickly observed that few tenured professors attended, whereas junior teaching staff participation was high. The latter group's need for a professional training program in university teaching was readily apparent, and as a result, since 2003 the University of Geneva has offered junior staff a comprehensive modular program in university teaching (Rege Colet & Barras, 2004). The program's modules are based on instructional design and constructive alignment: communication skills, learning outcomes, learning process and motivation, student assessment, and teaching evaluation. Each module is organized around a week of courses followed by two months of individual counseling. The faculty developers in charge of the program monitor the progress of participants in their everyday teaching and evaluate how they integrate knowledge and skills into their teaching practice. Participants are expected to design a course implementing strategies and tactics developed during the training week. Each module leads to a certificate if the candidate fulfills the assessment requirements. The modules end with a half-day debriefing session focusing on reflective practice during which participants can consider their own learning process and professional development.

Training teaching assistants is considered an educational and professional development project. The modular teaching program and the doctoral programs comprise the two pillars of professional development, the first dealing with teaching activities and the second with research activities in a knowledge-based economy. A project concept for doctoral programs developed by the universities of Geneva and Lausanne, has been adopted by all French-language universities. This project deals with the quality of research doctoral students conduct and the supervision they receive, but it also offers advice in career planning. Many of the programs enable doctoral students to attend teaching workshops that give formal recognition toward obtaining their degree. Specific workshops on communication skills, career management, work organization, appealing for funds, etc., are given regularly and attended eagerly. Faculty developers carry out most of the generic skills workshops, and participants in teacher training programs appreciate the individual counseling they get and now expect the same type of mentoring for their research supervision. This has encouraged closer collaboration between faculty developers and doctoral supervisors to discuss and share views about professional development.

For several years, The University of Fribourg has offered a similar postgraduate course in continuous education that is open to all staff, although the majority of participants are teaching assistants (*Centre de didactique universitaire et nouvelles technologies et enseignement*, 2009). Similar to the Geneva program, this program, called "Formation Did@cTIC," emphasizes instructional design but also pays attention to professional development and all forms of academic work. One of its components includes issues such as academic responsibilities, institutional constraints, and career management; a second component is instructional design; and a third component is student and teaching evaluation. The program is partly online using a blended-learning model, which gives students the opportunity to experience use of ICT in teaching and learning.

Introducing ICT into teaching and learning has also opened up opportunities for educational development. The additional funding linked to the SVC has enabled most universities to design a strategic plan for developing what is now referred to as e-learning. After a period of relative freedom in the choice of ICT tools, the universities were obliged to settle on one institutional platform and build up their e-learning policy. A new set of workshops surfaced in this context, concentrating on issues linked to the use of ICT in teaching and learning, while offering practical advice about teaching with the institutional platform. There is still a naive belief (Lebrun, 2005) that teaching models will change radically with the use of technology, and that the conceptual shift most educators have been awaiting will finally take place. Nevertheless, these workshops remain occasions for discussing teaching practice and encouraging academics to invest in their teaching.

Building the Community of Faculty Developers

One of the outcomes of implementing faculty development centers in universities is the growth of a community of faculty developers. Although the profession is not widely known or recognized, a number of people are working actively in the field and consider themselves faculty developers (Rege Colet, 2006). Achieving the Réseau CFE network was a first step toward acknowledging this emerging profession. However, interest in this professional field extends beyond the regions and, over the past years, has attracted national attention. In the late 1990s, people working in various support centers suggested regular meetings to get to know one another and share experiences. These meetings quickly confirmed the existence of a "community of practice" as defined by Wenger (1998) where faculty developers could share principles and values, recognize mutual practices and expertise, imagine building a common framework, and discuss promotion of faculty development in universities. This led to the launching of the SFDN in 2001.

During its first years, SFDN concentrated on coordinating meetings and organizing workshops for professional development of faculty developers. It issued two statement papers to establish a common framework. The first paper (SFDN, 2001) set out the underpinning principles and values of faculty development programs, inspired largely by a similar paper produced by the English-language Swiss Education Development Association (SEDA).

The framework emphasized the importance of understanding the learning process and of designing courses that align learning outcomes, teaching methods, and assessment. The second paper (SFDN, 2002) proposed guidelines for organizing faculty development activities. Both papers have contributed to affirming a new professional identity. Their purpose is to help individual centers build models and set common criteria for assessing and implementing activities.

The network became an official body in 2004 during the Bologna process. Early members of SFDN often commented on a general lack of institutional recognition of their work. Compounding this was the impression that the work groups established in the course of the Bologna process were not drawing on the expertise of faculty developers to meet the objectives of national guidelines. Becoming an official body was seen as a way of giving more voice to expertise built over the years and taking part in the process of change.

SFDN objectives are still related to faculty development and teaching and learning activities, but the organization now places more weight on promoting and obtaining recognition of faculty professional development. The agenda is to reinforce existing networks, contact national and international bodies active in the field, take part in national discussions on higher education, and place faculty development on the map of higher-education policy.

SFDN started by obtaining recognition of the CRUS. Places are now allocated for members in various work groups and steering committees, and invitations are issued for workshops and conferences. Much remains to be done within individual universities on institutional strategies, but faculty developers accept that the process is evolving. Everyday actions, published research results, and sound surveys on university teaching and learning will eventually clear the fog that now surrounds faculty development and will help to build academic and institutional recognition. For the time being, it seems that endorsement and empowerment lie in the hands of faculty developers who plead for a strong community of practice.

Next Steps and Challenges

The first step toward asserting faculty development and supporting new strategies in educational development is to obtain recognition of faculty development and its contribution to the quality of higher education. This means conceptualizing faculty development in the context of universities and establishing a framework. Explicit references to international expertise in the field and developing international networks sharing the same objectives will support work in this direction.

The need for a coherent framework on educational development is slowly becoming more apparent, not only to universities but also to policy-makers at the federal level. However, after eight years of generous funding, the federal program SVC is coming to an end because of a perceived lack of convincing results. Most evaluations conclude that introducing ICT was not sufficient to promote innovative teaching; more critical voices claim that the entire program was a waste of money. The most damaging effect of this unfortunate outcome is the dubious view some academics and policymakers now hold about educational development and pedagogical innovation. Faculty development centers have a difficult time explaining the work they carry out—a hard lesson on the need to report on their activities through evidence-based knowledge.

Fortunately, two other major changes will open up new avenues for educational development. First, future federal funding will go toward promoting doctoral programs that support developing skills required for a career as a researcher in a knowledge-based economy. Teaching in higher education is considered to be an important component of professional development, so educational development activities included in doctoral training will likely broaden. Second, the State Secretariat for Education and Research intends to reform the accreditation process and submit all higher-education institutions (both traditional universities and universities of applied sciences) to audits of their internal quality assurance systems. National guidelines based on European standards and guidelines for quality assurance (European Association for Quality Assurance in Higher Education, 2005) will be approved that emphasize quality of programs and teaching, thereby pushing higher education further up on the agenda. Federal funding is expected to be linked eventually to the outcomes of accreditation procedures.

The pressure for recognition of quality and teaching effectiveness will likely shed a positive light on educational development units and their staff. Nonetheless, higher-education institutions will have to tackle several issues to meet expectations. For a start, they will need to address initial and continuous education of faculty developers in universities immediately. The professional skills of staff working in such units and the academic value of their work will have to be addressed to achieve credibility in academic environments. Continuous education is slowly taking place through individual initiatives and network activities, but attendance is low. At present, no university has dared proposing a full academic program on university teaching. There is hope that the existence of similar programs at universities in other countries might encourage greater investment in the field.

Faculty development units will have to prepare for structural changes to gain institutional visibility and credibility. A stronger link with academic structures is a most likely outcome of these coming reforms. In this context, centers will be inclined to apply for external evaluation, not only to obtain external recognition of their work but also to be measured against international standards and criteria. Going through an external evaluation and taking part in a follow-up process focusing on professional capacity is another big challenge awaiting faculty development units.

External evaluation will bring to light the need to assess existing programs in teacher training. Furthermore, it is quite likely that accreditation will become necessary to obtain recognition of certifications issued by various institutions. Universities in Switzerland are beginning to recognize that the labor market for researchers is no longer limited to the location of study or home country. The market is becoming international, and professional mobility is expected in the course of an academic career. At the moment, candidates applying to universities in Switzerland are not required to provide evidence of their teaching skills as may be the case in other countries. In the future, candidates from Switzerland applying outside the country may be turned down if they cannot show sufficient expertise in teaching, or if their certification is not recognized. The new doctoral programs are an attempt to address this issue. Nonetheless, standards for educational or professional development activities will have to be set. A challenge for existing faculty development centers will be to use the expertise gained over the years in training junior staff to set up standards and criteria first, and then in getting their programs through the evaluation process. The larger challenge will be to convey principles and values that genuinely support teaching and learning in higher education and advocate the benefits of educational development in higher education.

Notes

1. Federal Institute of Technology, Lausanne; University of Fribourg; University of Geneva; University of Lausanne; and University of Neuchâtel.

2. Editors' note: Marcel Goldschmidt can be credited with initiating the faculty development movement in Switzerland. He completed his doctoral studies at Berkeley in the 1960s at a time when new teaching development centers were being created across North American campuses to address student discontent with the quality of teaching. Before returning to Switzerland, however, he started his career as an assistant professor at McGill University, and during this period he was instrumental in implementing the university's directive to form the Centre for Learning Development.

3. *Réseau romand de conseil, formation et évaluation pour l'enseignement universitaire* (CFE).

References

Biggs, J. (1999). *Teaching for quality learning at university.* Buckingham, UK: Society for Research into Higher Education and Open University Press.

Biggs, J. (2002). *Aligning the curriculum to promote good learning: The idea and ideals of constructive alignment.* Paper presented at the Constructive Alignment in Action: Imaginative Curriculum Symposium.

Centre de didactique universitaire et nouvelles technologies et enseignement (CDUNTE). (2009). Formation Did@cTIC [Did@cTIC training]. Retrieved from http://www.unifr.ch/didactic/assets/files/didactic/Brochure_2009-2010_fr.pdf.

Centre of Accreditation and Quality Assurance of the Swiss Universities (OAQ). (2005). Academic accreditation in Switzerland. Retrieved from www.oaq.ch/pub/en/03_01_00_akkredit_hochschul.php.

Conférence universitaire suisse occidentale (CUSO). (2003). Ecoles doctorales: principes généraux [Doctoral schools: General principles].

Durand, N. (2005, September). *Ateliers de formation pédagogique offerts aux enseignants : Quel est le profil du consommateur-type?* [Pedagogical development workshops for faculty: Which is the profile of the typical consumer?]. Paper presented at the 22nd Conference of the Association Internationale de Pédagogie Universitaire [International association on university teaching and learning], Geneva, Switzerland.

Elen, J. (2005). *The relationship between research and teaching in LERU-universities.* Unpublished draft research project, Katholieke Universiteit Leuven.

European Association for Quality Assurance in Higher Education. (2005). *Standards and guidelines for quality assurance in the European higher education area.* Helsinki: Author.

Kember, D., & Kwan, K. (2002). Lecturers' approaches to teaching and their relationship to conceptions of teaching. In N. Hativa & P. Goodyear (Eds.), *Teacher thinking, beliefs and knowledge in higher education* (pp. 219–239). Dordrecht, The Netherlands: Kluwer.

Knight, P. (2002). A systemic approach to professional development: Learning as practice. *Teaching and Teacher Education, 18*(3), 23–41.

Knight, P., & Trowler, P. R. (2001). *Departmental leadership in higher education.* Buckingham, UK: Society for Research into Higher Education and Open University.

Kreber, C. (1997). Evaluation of instructional development programs in Ontario universities. *Higher Education Perspectives, 1*(1), 23–41.

Lebrun, M. (2005). *eLearning pour enseigner et apprendre. Allier pédagogie et technologie* [E-learning for teaching and learning: An alliance between pedagogy and technology]. Louvain-La-Neuve, Belgium: Academia-Bruylant.

Ministry of Education and Research of Norway. (2005). *From Berlin to Bergen and beyond.* Retrieved from http://www.bologna-bergen2005.no/.

Prosser, M., & Trigwell, K. (1999). *Understanding learning and teaching: The experience in higher education.* Buckingham, UK: Society for Research into Higher Education and Open University.

Rege Colet, N. (2006). Représentations et modèles pédagogiques des conseillers pédagogiques en milieu universitaire [Representations and educational models of the educational developers in universities]. In N. Rege Colet & M. Romainville (Eds.), *La pratique enseignante en mutation à l'université* [Change of teaching practice in universities] (pp. 185–198). Bruxelles, Belgium: De Boeck.

Rege Colet, N. (2008). D'une communauté de praticiens à un programme de recherche. Quelques réflexions sur le développement de la pédagogie universitaire en Suisse romande [From a community of practitioners to a research program: Some reflections on the development of educational development in French-speaking Switzerland]. *Revue des Sciences de l'Education, 34*(3), 623–641.

Rege Colet, N., & Barras, H. (2004, May). *Préparer les assistants débutants à l'enseignement universitaire. Un programme de formation: principes et cadre de travail* [Preparing beginning TAs to teach in universities: A training program: Principles and working framework]. Paper presented at the 21st Conference of the Association Internationale de Pédagogie Universitaire [International association on university teaching and learning], Marrakesh, Morocco.

Rege Colet, N., & Durand, N. (2004). Working on the Bologna Declaration: Promoting integrated curriculum development and fostering conceptual change. *The International Journal for Academic Development, 9*(2), 167–170.

Rege Colet, N., Ricci, J.-L., Paulino, E., & Berthiaume, D. (2006). *Cadre de travail du Réseau CFE* [Working framework of the CFE Network].

Réseau CFE. (2005). *Convention des universités de Genève, Lausanne et Neuchâtel et de l'EPFL* [Convention of universities of Geneva, Lausanne, Neuchâtel and EPFL]. Retrieved from http://www.unil.ch/webdav/site/rcfe/shared/Doc_Rcfe/Convention-ReseauCFE-2005.pdf.

State Secretariat for Education and Research. (2005). *The federalist education system in Switzerland.* Retrieved from www.sbf.admin.ch/htm/bildung/bildung-e.html.

Swiss Faculty Development Network (SFDN). (2001). *Towards effective teaching and learning in Swiss universities.* Retrieved from http://www.unige.ch/formev/sfdn/documents.html.

Swiss Faculty Development Network (SFDN). (2002). *Towards effective training of faculty in Swiss universities.* Retrieved from www.sfdn.unige.ch.

Swiss Virtual Campus. (2005). Consolidation programme.

Trigwell, K. (2003). A relational approach model for academic development. In H. Eggins & R. Macdonald (Eds.), *The scholarship of academic development* (pp. 23–33). Buckingham, UK: Society for Research into Higher Education and Open University.

Weimer, M. (1990). *Improving college training.* San Francisco, CA: Jossey-Bass.

Wenger, E. C. (1998). *Communities of practice: Learning, meaning and identity.* New York: Cambridge University.

Wright, W. A. (Ed.). (1995). *Teaching improvement practices: Successful strategies for higher education.* Bolton, MA: Anker.

3

DANISH FACULTY
DEVELOPMENT STRATEGIES

Anette Kolmos

I n Scandinavia, faculty development as an institutionalized activity to improve the quality of teaching and learning is a relatively new field of endeavor. In the 1960s and '70s, ad hoc and random training courses were available; however, these were not institutionalized. It was in the late 1980s that the first centers for faculty development were established in Norway and soon thereafter in Sweden and Denmark.

One should view this evolution in Denmark within the general context of development of universities, which, as elsewhere in the world, has been affected by profound changes in social conditions. Until the 1970s, traditional universities dominated the scene, and higher education was an option only for the elite. However, at the beginning of that decade, with an increase in the number of students, the system was forced to expand (Bowden, 2003). Two new universities with problem- and project-based learning (PBL) pedagogy, Aalborg University and Roskilde University, were established. These universities turned out to be success stories, and they have had an incredible influence on higher-education development. Other higher-education institutions followed and shifted, in both small- and large-scale ways, toward student-centered learning. They incorporated case studies, problem- and project-based learning, cooperative learning, etc., into their curriculum to meet demographic challenges, but more importantly, to address concerns about student dropout rates and the quality of learning. At the same time, allocation of resources to higher education became linked more directly to the number of graduates and performance as determined by external evaluations conducted by national ministry organizations.

During the 1990s, higher-education institutions placed on their agendas lifelong learning, new graduate competencies, and internationalization and globalization. Employability also became a primary concern, and institutions began placing greater emphasis on the qualifications and ability of graduates to enter the waiting labor market. To achieve this goal, higher-education institutions increased cooperation with industry. These developments permitted a potential shift in attention to observable competencies, or behaviors, rather than to cognitive competencies, or analytical understanding. At the same time, they introduced the risk of characterizing conceptualization and formulation in strictly behavioral terms (Carter, Eriksen, Horst, & Troelsen, 2003). There have been expressions of concern about this potential outcome, and some have asserted the importance of maintaining a critical approach to the production of knowledge and competencies as part of lifelong learning and continuous education (Barnett, 1996; Bowden & Marton, 1998). As measures of accountability become more entrenched with changing management structures and the rise in private sector funding of universities, this concern may become even more pronounced. One manifestation of this changing trend is seen in a change in how academic leaders are appointed. Whereas in the past, democratic elections were held for this purpose, a new statute implemented in 2003–2004 has resulted in external appointments to senior university administration positions (vice chancellors, deans, and heads of departments) on university boards. This has led to closer links between academia and industry and non-academic organizations, but the potential impact of this relationship and the composition of new management teams on academic institutions in general and faculty development in particular is yet unknown.

Decentralized Faculty Development Strategies

Faculty development strategies as practiced in various countries comprising Scandinavia have much in common. In Norway, Sweden, and Denmark, pedagogical staff development is compulsory. Although each country expresses it through different rules and regulations, university teachers in each country have to obtain pedagogical qualifications (Kolmos, Vinther,

Andersson, Malmi, & Fuglem, 2004; Ministry of Science Technology and Development, 2000). There is, however, no common national certification.

The three Scandinavian countries also practice a nationally decentralized strategy for faculty development (Kolmos, 2004; Kolmos et al., 2004; Kolmos, Rump, Ingemarsson, Laloux, & Winther, 2001). This means that each institution in the respective country can fullfil formal requirements in whatever way it determines to be appropriate to meet specific content and process objectives. An important advantage of a decentralized strategy is that it involves the individual institution to a great extent, and management and staff are directly responsible for making policy decisions with the knowledge that they can adjust the content of training to match specific institutional needs. For example, if an institution has adopted a particular learning method, such as problem-based learning, it can orient its faculty development activities toward effective implementation of this approach.

Nationally decentralized strategies, however, also have disadvantages. For instance, they attach different meanings to certification. This, to some extent, can be addressed within national borders since variations in institutional culture are more or less known. Internationally, however, differences in meaning are likely to cause problems, particularly in the long run, because there will be too many and too specific certification processes in place at a time when accreditation based on specific criteria is becoming both a necessity and increasingly mandatory. An example where certification is given a common meaning and value is in Baden Württemberg, Germany, where the ministry has initiated a universal certificate program for all university teachers affiliated with universities in this region (Brendel, Kaiser, & Macke, 2004). The ministry is funding this initiative for five years but expects the universities to take over the responsibility of sustaining the program. Although sustained funding may be a challenge, it is anticipated that, at the end of the five years, a common certification process will be in place as will corresponding functional organization. Within this context, the extent to which faculty development can influence successful implementation of such a centrally generated policy will depend on institutional leadership.

Decentralized strategies have another potential disadvantage in that they may render faculty development centers more vulnerable at the local leadership level, particularly if there is a change in views about the importance of faculty development. In Denmark, there have already been instances of unit closures or reorganization because some centers were not included or did not participate in the newly defined institutional policy. In a period that is characterized by the establishment of new management teams and external boards, there is considerable uncertainty in the shape institutions will develop and the contributing role of faculty development to the process.

Yet another disadvantage is that central administrations characterize most faculty development centers as units that do not have a research mandate (Kolmos et al., 2004). This renders them less credible as faculty members in general tend to have little respect for university staff who do not conduct research in the same way they do. More important, however, at least at present, is the reality that faculty development staff lack sufficient knowledge in specific fields to perform rigorous research and document the impact of their roles. Having a service mandate does have positive dimensions though. A service mandate is less costly for the institution, and units may be located near the vice chancellor's office, since in this configuration, they are organizationally part of administration.

If faculty development is to play a more active part in the development of university culture, it needs to have an action-oriented research base that can document improvements and change processes. This approach takes into account learning theories related to communities of practice, reflection, and experimentation (Schön, 1983; Wenger, 1998) and implies not only faculty development units doing research on processes of change, but also teachers doing research on their subject specialties and teaching practices. Elements of this notion can be found in the Scandinavian faculty development culture, which may form the basis of further changes in Denmark. For that to happen, Denmark would need organizational integration, research-based courses that focus on ways of studying participants' everyday work life, and careful planning. One particular caution is the tensions that action-oriented research may cause within the research community. Danish research centers that are part of the Department of Education have research obligations and they tend to focus primarily on theory-driven rather than applied research. The different approaches between theory-driven and applied/action research create conflicts among researchers and make it particularly difficult for faculty developers to interact with their own colleagues. On the one hand, they have to deal with resistance among teaching staff and, on the other, they must justify their research approach to them. Indeed, faculty development staff often find themselves trapped between two opposing demands: a demand for the application of their work and a demand for the theoretical development of their discipline. As is the case in any newly developed field and research area, it will take time to establish a clear profile of expertise and competence in faculty development that can accommodate both aspects (Brew, 1998; Kolmos et al., 2004; Webb, 1998). Until then, any approach has to take into account the fragile balance between practice and theory and try to maintain it.

Centers and Networks

Denmark has 11 universities, the majority of which run their own faculty development centers. Some universities run subject centers, some of which are at the faculty level (for example, center for humanities and center for natural science). In addition to institutional units, there are several networks: two specifically focused on faculty development and one more generally focused on university pedagogy.

Centers of Faculty Development

The centers were established during the 1990s, and most still exist (Table 3.1). Their main activity is to plan and implement mandatory training for assistant professors and basic training courses for newer faculty such as PhD students and part-time teachers. In addition, the centers are involved in developing curricula and arranging seminars and conferences.

Those institutions that have opted not to establish faculty development centers purchase courses developed by others to fulfill the requirement of offering mandatory training for assistant professors. However, the experience from these institutions shows that it can be very difficult to adapt training that has been developed for a particular context to other subjects or differing institutional cultures. Therefore, the tendency is for each institution to establish its own center.

Missions of faculty development centers vary depending on whether they operate within an academic department, such as a Department of Education, or as part of the central administration of the university. In the former situation, the mission is both service and research; in the latter, it is only service. There is no clear trend toward either centralization or decentralization of units; we see examples of both occurring. For instance, the Technical University of Denmark moved a well-established unit from the research department to central administration, whereas Aalborg University moved a

TABLE 3.1
Faculty Development Centers

Technical University of Denmark	Danmarks Tekniske Videncenter: http://www.dtv.dk/
Copenhagen Business School	CBS Learning Lab: http://www.ll.cbs.dk/
Copenhagen University	Pædagogisk Center Samfundsvidenskab: http://www.samf.ku.dk/ Formidlingscentert på Humaniora: http://www.hum.ku.dk/
Roskilde University Center	Institut for Uddannelsesforskning: http://www.educ.ruc.dk/
University of Southern Denmark	Center for universitetspædagogik: http://www.sdu.dk/Adm/CFE/
Aalborg University	Pædagogisk Udviklingscenter, Ålborg Universitet: http://www.puc.aau.dk/ UCPBL: http://www.ucpbl.org/ E-learning lab Nordjylland: http://www.ell.aau.dk/
Aarhus University	Universitetspædagogisk Udviklingsenhed: http://www.au.dk/da/rektor/paedagog/ Enhed for Medicinsk Uddannelse: http://www.medu.au.dk/ Center for Undervisningsudvikling: http://www.humaniora.au.dk/index.jsp
Royal Veterinary and Agricultural University of Denmark	IT Learning Center: http://www.kvl.dk/

unit from central administration to the Department of Learning and Education.

Newer teachers accept the concept of faculty development more readily than senior academics (professors and associate professors) do. Newer teachers stress the need for learning techniques and methods to handle changing circumstances. Without pedagogical training, the only tools available to them are those they have seen their own teachers apply. Senior staff may have negative conceptions about faculty development and to change that, current practices must change. This can happen through the introduction of new ideas and training in planning and carrying out teaching and the dissemination of research findings on various dimensions of faculty development.

To find out about the success of faculty development practices, the Danish Evaluation Institute (2003) (http://www.eva.dk) has conducted an evaluation of two centers: the Technical University of Denmark and the Copenhagen Business School. This evaluation found that center success depends on institutional factors: relationships with managers, general level of acceptance of pedagogical issues, and openness to work with teaching and learning. The evaluation report stresses the importance of managerial support of faculty development units, especially when conflicting goals within the university culture may be potential barriers. These could comprise, for instance:

- priority given to research;
- view of teaching as an individual process; or
- career advancement trajectories if considered as administrative adjuncts.

Exercises such as this evaluation can have consequences. For instance, as a result of this report, one of the evaluated universities moved its unit out of the academic department in which it was located, arguing that further funding for more research was not forthcoming. The opposing argument could have also been made to make more research funds available to the unit. The decision made in this case was clearly the top management's, and it underscores the extent to which institutional leadership can influence the promotion of faculty development.

Pedagogical Network

To create qualified staff developers, several national networks have been established. Most of these networks rely on bottom-up strategies that support the exchange of experiences. Founded in the late 1990s, the Danish Network for University Pedagogy (DUN) (http://www.dun-net.dk/Center.asp) is the umbrella organization for all universities in the country and is a member of the International Consortium for Educational Development (ICED), an international organization for all national networks in the field of pedagogical training in higher education. DUN arranges annual conferences and seminars and runs a newly established online journal on university pedagogy.

Another network is the National Pedagogical Network for Engineering Education (IPN) (http://www.ipn.dk). It was founded in 1996 to ensure the quality of pedagogical and curriculum development activities of Danish engineering education institutions—universities and colleges. IPN was originally intended as a three-year project, but it received a fourth-year extension ending in 2003. Today IPN is funded by all institutions that have engineering education (Vinther & Kolmos, 2002).

The objective of IPN is to strengthen the development of pedagogical and didactic quality in engineering education by:

- coordinating pedagogical and curriculum development activities;
- providing training and education for part-time teachers, PhD students, assistant professors, associate professors, and professors;
- collecting and disseminating information concerning pedagogy;
- initiating curriculum development projects at the institutional level; and
- creating a forum for exchange of ideas and experiences at institutional, national, and international levels.

IPN is one of Denmark's success stories in higher education. Since 1996, the network has managed to run comprehensive training activities for all engineering education institutions in Denmark.

The Center for Educational Development in University Science (DCN) (http://www.dcn.aau.dk) is a similar pedagogical network whose main purpose is to build a basis of pedagogical and educational competencies for education in natural science at universities. This network was established to create centers at institutions and provide funds for establishing curriculum development projects and training courses, including comprehensive PhD programs for qualifying staff developers in this field. The network is funded by the Ministry of Research and has had a margin of success, as evidenced by established subject centers at Copenhagen University, Aarhus University, and Aalborg University.

Experiences of Danish faculty developers indicate that institutional strategies and national networks are essential to renew knowledge, organize activities across institutional boundaries, and stay up-to-date on international activities. For relatively small centers such as the ones in Denmark, a national network is a necessary element in faculty development.

Mandatory Training

The primary strategy for staff development involves compulsory courses for assistant professors who hold this position if they have a PhD. Assistant professors are eligible to apply for an associate professorship (a permanent position) after three years. If they do so, they must document that they have had pedagogical training equivalent to that of an assistant professor. Before this requirement was put in place, it was difficult to motivate university teachers involved in research to participate in lengthy pedagogical development courses. Since 1994, in principle, no associate professor without pedagogical training has been employed.

With this policy in place, the position of assistant professorship can be very stressful. After finalizing a PhD thesis, assistant professors have to start new research projects. To obtain an associate professorship, they must also demonstrate excellent teaching skills. This timing for compulsory pedagogical training is less than ideal, but if it is to have an impact on decisions pertaining to permanent appointments, such a schedule offers the only window of opportunity (Petersen, 2005).

Mandatory training takes 175 to 200 hours and happens under the supervision of a senior colleague from the participant's department. Training is implemented in different forms applying differing models; most institutions have used teaching portfolios for the past seven years. Variation among models is primarily at the implementation rather than conceptual level—depending on, for instance, if participants attend workshops within or outside their own institution (Kolmos et al., 2001). Common objectives that cut across formats are to develop understanding of the teaching and learning processes in order to set aims for teaching. Similarly, to develop an understanding of variations in student approaches to learning; to obtain an overview of various teaching, learning, and assessment models; to develop a basic understanding of concepts of learning and how it is achieved; and to be able to analyze learning situations and the level of students' prior knowledge.

Teachers cannot acquire many or most of the required competencies simply by reading books. They have to learn them through training and experience, so the competencies can be best facilitated through a structured approach where teachers learn to analyze and plan their teaching, and where they receive feedback in various ways in authentic teaching contexts. A teacher can also learn how to renew and build on teaching practices by establishing and evaluating teaching experiments.

The development of specific pedagogical competencies can also be a topic worthy of research. As in scientific research, findings about teaching and learning can be disseminated through formal presentations at conferences. More importantly, research findings can provide greater insight and awareness of learning processes that can in turn inform teaching practice. After all, research involves learning and an increased awareness of the learning process can also contribute to an increased understanding of the research process.

Many consider that it is through research that academics develop into competent experts, but it is also possible to develop competencies through teaching. The basic premise in both contexts is that training in and learning about the core competencies (communication, project management, learning, collaboration, and the like) will influence both research and teaching, no matter where and how they are developed. Faculty development can support this approach. In addition to developing specific knowledge about learning and teaching, faculty development also involves changing a strongly held belief that once one becomes a researcher, an associate professor, or a professor, one no longer needs continuing education. The reality could not be further from the truth: one can be a professor without knowing anything about teaching. Taking initiatives to learn about teaching, even at accomplished stages of one's academic career, not only benefits the individual, but sets a good leadership example of lifelong learning.

Institutional Strategy at Aalborg University

Since 1994 more than 300 assistant professors have completed the compulsory training course in pedagogy at Aalborg University. Introducing it has contributed to success in making staff development a subject for discussion, and especially in preparing the groundwork for establishing curriculum development projects and subject-based pedagogical courses. From this experience, one could conclude that compulsory education should be considered as an essential part of a strategy to develop an integrated pedagogical culture.

The overall goal of this training course is to enable assistant professors to better reflect on their own teaching and learning practices, and to further develop their teaching methods and the learning approaches of their students (Kolmos & Krogh, 2003a). Spread over three semesters, the course involves four combination modules, alternating theory and practical applications

(Table 3.2). An assistant professor's time investment is estimated at about 175 working hours—calculated as part of the teaching load during the period appointed as assistant professor.

The basic objectives of the course are to:

- develop knowledge of basic university pedagogy and didactics, focusing on abilities to develop, plan, design, and analyze various types of educational programs (for example, lectures, seminars, study groups, and project work);
- develop knowledge and understanding of learning theories to become capable of initiating learning processes among a variety of students, both individually and in groups;
- become familiar with a variety of pedagogic "tools" and methods, including technologically supported education to be able to draw from didactic analysis when applying tools to various student target groups;
- strengthen project-advising competencies in relation to initiation and support of students' group processes;
- obtain knowledge and understanding of evaluation as a developmental and "control" tool to be able to implement various types of evaluations with students and, furthermore, to develop abilities of self-evaluation;
- develop skills in supervising colleagues; and
- gain experience by working with experiments and methods of reflection for teaching portfolios (Kolmos & Krogh, 2003a).

The four-module course is organized with a mix of theoretical considerations, practical experiences, and reflection. Various types of planned activities relate to the modules (Table 3.2).

Each assistant professor is assigned two advisors: one from the Center for University Teaching and Learning (CUTL) and a practical advisor assigned by the assistant professor's own department and formally appointed by the department head (Figure 3.1).

The basic objectives of advisory activities are to:

- create new opportunities for future activities through the development of deeper insight into and understanding of an assistant professor's own subject- and teaching-oriented potential;

TABLE 3.2
Overview of Training for Assistant Professors

Module	Dates	Objectives	Activities and Portfolios
Module 1	October–January	• Initiate reflection on one's own pedagogic and didactic course frames relating to one's own teaching practices; formulate expectations, pedagogic problem proposals, and goals for participation in the course	• Workshop, study group, readings • Submission of first version of portfolio with reflection on experiences
Module 2	February–July	• Gain teaching skills in relation to various types of teaching and situations • Obtain ability to reflect didactically, including ability to evaluate one's own teaching, and to establish goals and methods for future development of teaching practices in subsequent work with portfolio • Develop ability to set up teaching experiments • Develop ability to evaluate and adopt constructive position regarding one's own and others' teaching, including ability to discuss pedagogy and course syllabus with colleagues and students	• Teaching, experimenting, receiving supervision • Activities related to portfolio and reflection

Module 3	August	• Gain knowledge of and ability to reflect on teaching and learning processes • Gain specific knowledge within chosen pedagogical and subject-related fields • Develop ability to formulate limited and realistic developmental goals for one's own teaching • Gain knowledge and experiences through observation, testing, and evaluation of one's own and others' teaching and advising	• Workshop • Objectives and reflection on last part of portfolio
Module 4	September–December	• Increase teaching proficiency within as broad a spectrum of teaching situations and types as possible • Develop ability to practice both pedagogic and didactic self-reflection in connection with one's own teaching, and establish realistic objectives for continued development and change of teaching practices • Develop ability to evaluate and adopt constructive position to one's own teaching, including discussion of pedagogic and didactic problem formulations with colleagues and students	• Teaching, experimenting, receiving supervision • Submitting final portfolio

FIGURE 3.1
Advisors for Assistant Professor

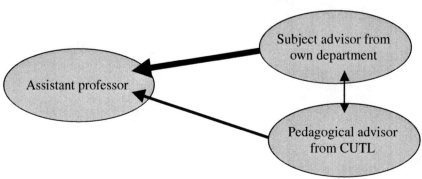

- provide opportunities to gain increased insight into potential blind spots of an assistant professor's planning, directing, conducting, and evaluating the teaching;
- provide response to the process of reflection and a teaching portfolio; and
- create new insights into and performance opportunities for supervision—in other words, foster the mutual nature of understanding as expressed by: "I become wiser concerning the other's teaching through my observations; at the same time, I also become wiser concerning my own teaching" (Kolmos & Krogh, 2003b).

The advisory process requires the interest, openness, loyalty, and integrity of all involved parties because of the tremendous implications for successful attainment of required qualifications that lead to the advancement of an individual's career. In concrete terms, advisory sessions encompass three main activities: introductory meeting, teaching observations, and follow-up counseling. Special workshops are available to subject advisors so they can practice feedback techniques. There is no concluding formal assessment. Instead, the two advisors write a statement conveying their judgment of whether the assistant professor passes. In reality, no assistant professor fails; for some, however, judgment may be less than complimentary.

Engaging staff from departments of assistant professors as advisors has been a great advantage in many ways. For one, because a subject advisor has to learn the same type of concepts as does an assistant professor, the number of participants in a given course has been double the number of assistant professors, and all subject advisors are invited to all workshops free of charge. Another advantage has been the tremendous benefit to the institution, particularly when senior staff members begin to discuss pedagogical issues. Because the role of advisor acknowledges a certain level of expertise and appeals to associate professors and professors, there has been no need to coerce them into participating in this project.

Despite obvious successes, however, internal evaluations of this model for staff development point to a number of difficulties. One is that academic units need to be sufficiently motivated to participate. This is a necessary condition; it isn't sufficient. Participants often find the courses too long and time for meetings with advisors too short when they still have to attend to their routine daily business.

Nevertheless, internal evaluations show that, in general, participants are satisfied with their experience. They especially emphasize the importance of the acquired learning tools and methods and believe that they can use them for planning and developing their teaching practices. In addition, they obtain a terminology that they can use effectively to discuss issues related to teaching and learning.

This partnership has a cost, which is easy to calculate. The first expense pertains to the time an assistant professor invests—the number of teaching hours or credits added to a teaching load. The second expense is the time of the advisor who is assigned the supervision activity as part of a teaching load. Finally, there are costs associated with running workshops. In total, the cost is around 10,000 to 12,000 Euros (the equivalent of USD 14,500 to 17,500) per participant, depending on rates of teaching hours.

Impact of Pedagogical Training

The effects of compulsory training are beginning to show in the system now that a new generation of managers (heads of departments and study boards) has taken the training. There is evidence that pedagogical training has had an impact on university culture and quality of teaching. Internal evaluations show that participants feel they have attained:

- mental models for analyzing new teaching and learning situations;
- language for discussing teaching and learning issues;

- tools for teaching processes;
- changes in teaching practices;
- impact on culture of departments—pedagogical topics have a place on the agenda, with discussions of teaching planning going on in coffee rooms as well as formal meetings; and
- success in establishing new projects—for instance, in information and communication technology (ICT).

Some years ago, Lunds Technical University (Sweden) undertook a massive endeavor, called the Breakthrough Project, that involved many activities, including special-interest seminars, campus conferences, team planning for teaching, educational consultancy, and pedagogical academy. The last included the development of teaching portfolios and a promise of raises upon completion and satisfactory assessment. Moreover, departments promised bonuses of additional annual subsidies. Evaluations of this project show that during and after the period there was an increase in the number of curriculum development projects, and discussion of and approaches to pedagogical issues were highly positive and favorable (Roxå & Andersson, 2004). Unfortunately, no follow-up studies were conducted on the direct impact on students' learning. This experience only underscores the importance of sustained vigilance in monitoring impact and effectiveness of faculty development initiatives.

New Pedagogical Challenges: Intercultural Learning

One key advantage of a decentralized structure is its greater flexibility in permitting content to be adjusted to specific institutional needs. In Denmark, the number of foreign students varies from one institution to another. At Aalborg University, for instance, more than one-third of all PhD students at the Doctoral School for Technology and Science are from abroad. The number of assistant professors coming from abroad, therefore, is also increasing. With rises in numbers of foreign students and assistant professors, master programs at Danish universities are likely to be taught in English within a few years. Few international students speak or understand Danish, and it is expected that university teachers will be able to teach in English and will have obtained sufficient intercultural understanding through their research to accommodate increasingly diverse groups of students.

However, these assumptions do not always correspond with reality. Reengaging in research does not mean that one understands intercultural learning. Reading international publications and visiting other countries for short stays does not necessarily promote cultural learning. The time, effort, and ability required to develop new educational programs or to adapt existing programs to new target groups can sometimes be overestimated. University staff who have mixed ethnic backgrounds do not automatically or necessarily collaborate to improve the quality of teaching. At the curriculum level, there are also some potential difficulties. Most curricula are currently overloaded with content without a clear vision of goals, and there are increasing expectations for development of new interdisciplinary curricula relating to changing social conditions. These new demands place unprecedented pressures on educational institutions as they try to position themselves nationally and internationally to attract students who are becoming increasingly savvy and demanding consumers (Bourgeois, 2002). A multicultural classroom is vastly different from a homogeneous classroom. It involves different traditions concerning learning as well as different experiences, knowledge, and capabilities that need to be taken into consideration when planning teaching. On the positive side, the potential of finding new ways to reach more students and increasing learning output motivates even senior staff to seek more training.

Formalizing Pedagogical Training

A recent Danish initiative is the establishment of a Master in Problem-Based Learning in Engineering and Science (http://www.mpbl.aau.dk/) within the context of which staff development is formalized (Figure 3.2). This program is available in distance format, so it can involve international participants from all over the world. Content is organized to fit problem- and project-based learning (PBL) methods in that participants have to experiment and develop their own teaching and curriculum. The overall intention of this program is to offer formalized training to change traditional education.

The first module of the program involves developing teaching portfolios in which participants reflect on previous and current teaching experiences and start to think about problem- and PBL. Progression through the program supports change in thinking and actions regarding teaching. This is done through:

FIGURE 3.2
Overview of the Master in Problem-Based Learning in Engineering and Science

Programme overview

Module 1 - Development of Teaching Competencies

• PBL in Engineering and Science Education • Learning Theory for Engineering and Science Education • IT and the Study Programme • Engineering Didactics	10 ECTS
• Project – Teaching Portfolio	5 ECTS

Module 2 - Planning of Teaching Experiments

• Intercultural Learning and PBL • Development of Process Competencies • Scientific Methods in Engineering	9 ECTS
• Project – Planning a Teaching Experiment	6 ECTS

Module 3 - Implementation of Teaching Experiments. Specialisation

• IT in Teaching • Evaluation and Quality Development in Engineering and Science Education • Strategies for Management and Staff Development • Supervision • Engineering Competencies in a Global Information Society • Work Based Learning • PBL and Mathematics	9 ECTS
• Project – Implementing a Teaching Experiment	6 ECTS

Module 4 - Reflection and Evaluation

• Research Methods	3 ECTS
• Project – Final Thesis	12 ECTS

- reflection on and development of teaching competencies to develop teaching experiments on a systemic level;
- a focus on project work and a gradual shift in teaching experiments from planning via implementation to evaluation; and
- a gradual shift from individual types of learning to group-based learning processes.

The core question surrounding this program is whether it is possible to achieve the same learning objectives at a distance. Evidence from the first pilot courses and their evaluation shows that running distance courses involves considerable challenges. However, participants seem to feel that they have improved their own practices and can apply ideas and methods learned from these courses. Although comparing learning outcomes between face-to-face training and this distance format is not yet possible, one can conclude that participants at a distance are facilitated in mini-projects and do improve their teaching practices (Kolmos, Du, Dahms, & Qvist, 2008). These types of programs add a very important dimension to faculty development as they create an international community of practice for reflection on and development of teaching and learning in higher education.

Concluding Perspectives

Faculty development is an important element in the development of universities. Danish (and Scandinavian) experiences show that faculty development:

- has an impact on teachers' approaches to teaching and learning and on the development of university cultures;
- is vulnerable, especially in decentralized contexts where its existence and growth depends on institutional leadership;
- requires a research dimension to renew knowledge and document effectiveness of faculty development; and
- can have an impact on both teaching and research.

For the future development of universities in Europe, where new demands for teaching and learning are constant—especially concerning the Bologna process and international mobility, there must be expertise to develop education. University staff members are not necessarily good teachers just because they have successful research careers. Research in subject areas does not provide insight into understanding learning and teaching; however, research that involves reflection on learning and teaching processes does. If staff development is to play a more active part in development of university cultures, there is need for action-oriented research approaches and documentation of processes of change and improvement. This means not only that faculty development units should research the processes of change, but that teachers also should research their own research and teaching processes. The highlighted initiatives in the faculty development culture of Denmark (and Scandinavia) offer ideas that can inform practices in other countries in Europe and North America.

References

Barnett, R. (1996). *The limits of competence: Knowledge, higher education and society.* Buckingham, UK: The Society for Research into Higher Education and Open University Press.

Bourgeois, E. (2002). *Higher education and research for the ERA: Current trends and challenges for the future.* Luxembourg: Office for Official Publications of the European Communities.

Bowden, J. (2003). Why do we need reforms, which and how do we implement them? In J. Carter, K. Eriksen, S. Horst, & R. Troelsen (Eds.), *If reform of science is the answer: What were the questions?* (pp. 9–28). Copenhagen, Denmark: University of Copenhagen, Center for Naturfagenes Didaktik.

Bowden, J., & Marton, F. (1998). *The university of learning.* London: Kogan Page.

Brendel, S., Kaiser, K., & Macke, G. (Eds.). (2004). *Hochschuldidaktische Qualifizierung: Strategien und Konzepte im internationalen Vergleich* [University didactic qualification: Strategies and concepts in international comparison] (Vol. 115). Bielefeld, Germany: W. Bertelsmann Verlag.

Brew, A. (1998). *Directions in staff development.* Buckingham, UK: Society for Research into Higher Education and Open University Press.

Carter, J., Eriksen, K., Horst, S., & Troelsen, R. (2003). *If reform of science is the answer: What were the questions?* Copenhagen, Denmark: University of Copenhagen, Center for Naturfagenes Didaktik.

Danish Evaluation Institute. (2003). *Vilkår for pædagogisk udviklingsarbejde— Evaluering af de pædagogiske enheder på DTU og CBS* [Conditions for educational development: Evaluation of faculty development units]. Copenhagen, Denmark: Evalueringsinstituttet.

Kolmos, A. (2004). Staff development strategies and knowledge society. In S. Brendel, K. Kaiser, & G. Macke (Eds.), *Hochschuldidaktische Qualifizierung: Strategien und Konzepte im internationalen Vergleich* [Qualifications for university didactics: Strategies and concepts in international comparison] (Vol. 115, pp. 41–52). Bielefeld, Germany: W. Bertelsmann Verlag.

Kolmos, A., Du, X., Dahms, M., & Qvist, P. (2008). Staff development for change to problem based learning. *International Journal of Engineering Education, 24*(4), 772–782.

Kolmos, A., & Krogh, L. (2003a). University pedagogy for assistant professors at Aalborg University (part 1). *Das Hochschulwesen, 1*, 37–44.

Kolmos, A., & Krogh, L. (2003b). University pedagogy for assistant professors at Aalborg University (part 2). *Das Hochschulwesen, 2*, 75–80.

Kolmos, A., Rump, C., Ingemarsson, I., Laloux, A., & Winther, O. (2001). Organization of staff development: Strategies and experiences. *European Journal of Engineering Education, 26*(4), 329–342.

Kolmos, A., Vinther, O., Andersson, O., Malmi, L., & Fuglem, M. (Eds.). (2004). *Faculty development in Nordic engineering education.* Aalborg, Denmark: Aalborg University.

Ministry of Science Technology and Development. (2000). *Notat om stillingsstruktur for videnskabeligt personale med forskningsopgaver og undervisningsopgaver ved universiteter m.fl. under Forskningsministeriet* [Note on career structure for academic staff with research and teaching duties at universities]. Copenhagen, Denmark: Forskningsministeriet.

Petersen, D. (2005). *Hvor svært kan det være? En kvalitativ analyse af Adjunktundersøgelsens åbne spørgsmål* [How difficult can it be? A qualitative analysis of the open questions in the study of assistant professors]. Aalborg, Denmark: Aalborg University, Institut for økonomi, politik og forvaltning.

Roxå, T., & Andersson, P. (2004). The breakthrough project: A large-scale project of pedagogical development. In A. Kolmos, O. Vinther, O. Andersson, L. Malmi, & M. Fuglem (Eds.), *Faculty development in Nordic engineering education* (pp. 25–48). Aalborg, Denmark: Aalborg University.

Schön, D. S. (1983). *The reflective practitioner: How professionals think in action.* New York: Basic Books.

Vinther, O., & Kolmos, A. (2002). National strategies for staff and faculty development in engineering education. *Global Journal of Engineering Education, 6*(2), 161–166.

Webb, G. (1998). *Understanding staff development.* Buckingham, UK: Society for Research into Higher Education and Open University.

Wenger, E. C. (1998). *Communities of practice: Learning, meaning and identity.* New York: Cambridge University Press.

4

FACULTY DEVELOPMENT IN BELGIAN UNIVERSITIES

Mieke Clement and Mariane Frenay

I n this chapter, we first provide a general overview of the structure and characteristics of Belgian higher education. Second, we describe the way in which Belgian universities define and enact faculty development. Third, we take a closer look at the basic assumptions of the teacher training and instructional development programs of two of the oldest centers for faculty development in Belgium: the educational support units of the Katholieke Universiteit Leuven (K.U. Leuven [Flanders]) and the Université catholique de Louvain (UCL [French-speaking community]). Fourth, we discuss actual challenges that these and other Belgian teaching development units are facing and how they are coping with these challenges. Last, we briefly reflect on the future of faculty development in Belgium.

Structure and Characteristics of Higher Education

Since 1988 education in Belgium has been regulated and for the most part financed by the French and Flemish linguistic communities. As a result, these two communities bear full responsibility for their respective education systems. Despite this linguistically imposed divide, as a result of an extended common history that spans from 1830 to 1987, higher education in the French- and the Flemish-speaking communities still shows strong common characteristics. Among the few areas of jurisdiction for education regulated by the national legislator that transcends linguistic borders is the number of years for mandatory schooling.

Structure of Higher Education

Article 24 of the Belgian constitution establishes the principle of freedom of teaching and provides for the existence of state-organized teaching contexts. Within this constitutional framework, two networks of institutions of higher education have developed: public institutions set up by the state and administered by either the linguistic communities or the provincial or municipal authorities and private institutions, the vast majority of which are denominational (Roman Catholic). Private institutions of higher education, if they meet well-defined conditions, receive financial aid from the state.

Higher education has a two-track system. Degrees are awarded either by *hautes écoles—hogescholen*[1] or by the universities. In the 2004–2005 academic year, the *hautes écoles* of the French community had 83,210 undergraduates (52.5% women), and the universities had approximately 65,400 students in undergraduate and graduate programs (57.7% women). In Flanders, for the same academic year, the higher-education institutions outside universities (*hogescholen*) had 104,995 undergraduates (54.8% women), and the universities had 57,005 students in undergraduate and graduate programs (55.5% women).

Access to Higher Education

Access to higher education is open to students who have successfully completed technical or comprehensive secondary education. There are, however, a few exceptions to this rule pertaining to programs that invoke *numerus clausus*; examples include programs in medicine and in engineering in the French-speaking jurisdiction, which impose an entrance examination for selection purposes. The open-access system has had three major consequences:

- the participation rate in higher education is 67.3%—20-year-olds in levels 5[2] and 6[3] of the International Standard Classification of Education (ISCED) in 2002–2003 (Eurostat, 2005)—which is relatively high;
- the success rate for first-year students who enter higher education is low;[4] and
- in some higher-education programs, there are huge differences in student demographics from year to year.

It is in this light that faculty members' pedagogical abilities and the extent to which they are prepared to address these consequences should be considered.

Teaching Staff

Academic staff in Belgian universities can have a range of appointments with varying teaching responsibility. They can be full-time in a tenure-track position;[5] part-time or sessional;[6] full-time senior researchers[7] (from the scientific community); full-time junior researchers (maximum teaching load of 20%); or full-time research and teaching assistants.

Consequences of the Bologna Declaration

From the time European ministers for education signed the Bologna Declaration (1999), Belgian higher education as a whole has engaged in a large-scale restructuring process. The aim of the Bologna Declaration is to create consistency in European higher education by 2010. To this end, several concrete objectives have been put forward, including creating a common frame of reference to understand and compare diplomas; restructuring programs at undergraduate (bachelor) and graduate (master) levels where an undergraduate diploma is relevant for the labor market and a prerequisite for a graduate program; implementing credit systems compatible with the European Credit Transfer and Accumulation System;[8] and establishing a trans-European dimension in quality assurance; and reducing impediments to student and teacher mobility.

The far-reaching impact of the Bologna Declaration, on both individual programs and institutions, has been documented (Clement, McAlpine, & Waeytens, 2004; Verhesschen & Verburgh, 2004), and higher-education institutions have been redesigning their curricula. Decrees on the structure of higher education have changed the diploma structure (March 31, 2004, for the French community; April 4, 2003, for the Flemish community). The former certificates of *candidature* or *kandidaturen* programs (120 ECTS credits) and *licence* or *licentiaat* programs (120 or 180 ECTS credits) have been replaced by bachelor (180 ECTS credits) and master degree programs (additional 60 or 120 ECTS credits). Today, in contrast to the previous undergraduate diploma, a bachelor diploma may have value in the labor market. It nonetheless remains to be seen how the job market eventually will react to holders of bachelor degrees from universities, who traditionally have entered the job market with a graduate diploma following four or five years of university studies.

One of the consequences of implementing the Bologna Declaration has been closely forged collaborations between universities and nonuniversity higher-education institutions. In Flanders, five associations, or *associaties*,[9] have been created that make it easier for students to transfer between institutions (for example, between universities and nonuniversities). However, in the French-speaking community, the decree on the structure of higher education has forced the nine universities to be part of three *académies*.[10] The role of these *académies*, as defined by the decree, extends beyond the creation of a network. Each *académie* is obliged to develop a common doctorate regulation (even if doctoral training is organized at the French-community level). Additionally, each is required to organize a *Centre de didactique supérieure* (CDIS) for promoting and coordinating actions to promote success in the first year at the bachelor level.

The goal of creating a European dimension in quality assurance and a common system for accreditation of higher-education programs has also demanded that greater attention be paid to the quality of education, including the quality of teaching staff. When the challenges facing curricular changes, the increasing demand for educational innovation, and the integration of technology are added to the mix, the need for appropriate educational and faculty development becomes apparent.

Faculty Development: An Overview

General Characteristics

Faculty development in Belgium can be described in terms of several dimensions, listed below[11] and explained in Table 4.1:

- structure/position: centralized or decentralized unit within the university and relationship to other higher-education institutions within the *associatie* or *académie*;
- mission: research and/or service;
- range of programs and initiatives;
- conceptual approach to teaching; and
- domains of development.

Flemish universities have created small-scale units at the central level of the university that function predominantly as service providers. The exceptions are K.U. Leuven and the University of Antwerp, where the units also

TABLE 4.1
Faculty Development Units

	Structure/Position	Mission	Programs and Initiatives	Teaching Philosophy	Development Domains
Flemish-Speaking Community					
Katholieke Universiteit Leuven (K.U.L.) (Leuven)	• Centralized • *Associatie*	• Services • Research	• Personal advice • Targeted: one-year program for faculty members; program for teaching assistants; workshops for program directors • General: workshops and information sessions for faculty members and teaching assistants • Tailor-made initiatives with(in) faculties	• Guided independent learning	• Instructional development • Educational innovation • Curriculum development • Quality assurance
Vrije Universiteit Brussels (VUB) (Brussels)	• Centralized • University only	• Services	• Personal advice • One-year program for faculty members • Workshops	• Competency-focused learning through flexible teaching	• Instructional development • Educational innovation
Universiteit Antwerpen (UA) (Antwerp)	• Centralized • *Associatie*	• Services • Research	• Lunchtime seminars • One-year program for faculty members • One-year program for teaching assistants	• Competency-focused learning through student-centered teaching	• Instructional development

Institution					
Universiteit Gent (UGent) (Ghent)	• Centralized • University only	• Services	• One-year program for faculty members • Follow-up workshops	• Information not available	• Open university • Permanent training • Information and communication technology (ICT) • Instructional development
Universiteit Hasselt (Uhasselt) (Hasselt)	• Centralized • University only	• Services	• Information not available	• Information not available	• Instructional development • Educational innovation
French-Speaking Community **• Académie Wallonie-Bruxelles**					
Université libre de Bruxelles (ULB) (Brussels)	Coordinating committee[1] 2001	• Services	• Workshops • Personal advice	• Information not available	• Information and communication technology (ICT) • Educational innovation
Université de Mons-Hainaut (UMH) (Mons)	Information not available	• Information not available	• Information not available	• Information not available	• Student guidance
Faculté polytechnique de Mons (FPMs) (Mons)	Information not available	• Information not available	• Information not available	• Information not available	• Student guidance

TABLE 4.1 (Continued)

	Structure/Position	Mission	Programs and Initiatives	Teaching Philosophy	Development Domains
• Académie Wallonie-Europe					
Université de Liège (ULG) (Liège)	Centralized: IFRES[2] 2005	• Services • Research	• Personal advice on evaluation, problem-based learning (PBL), and distance learning • Training for newly appointed faculty and teaching assistants • One-year program for faculty members—since 2002 (DES-FORMASUP)[3]	• Information not available	• Teaching policy • Research in higher education • Information and communication technology (ICT) • Instructional development
Faculté universitaire des sciences agronomique de Gembloux (Fsagx) (Gembloux)	Information not available	• Information not available	• Information not available	• Information not available	• Student guidance
• Académie universitaire Louvain					
Université catholique de Louvain (UCL) (Louvain-la-Neuve)	Centralized	• Services • Research	• Personal advice • Teaching support • Lunchtime seminars • Workshops • One-year program for faculty members—since 2002 (DES)	• *Gérer sa formation:* • Autonomous learning through student-centered teaching and autonomous learning	• Instructional development • Support for teaching and evaluation • Educational innovation • Curriculum development and evaluation • Information and communication technology (ICT)

Institution					
Facultés universitaires Notre-Dame de la Paix (FuNDP) (Namur)	• Centralized[4] • University only	• Services • Research	• Personal advice • Teaching support • Newsletter	• Information not available	• Student guidance • Information and communication technology (ICT) • Instructional development
Facultés universitaires Saint-Louis (FUSL) (Brussels)	• Information not available		• Information not available	• Information not available	• Student guidance
Facultés universitaires catholiques de Mons (FUCAM) (Mons)	• Information not available		• Information not available	• Information not available	• Student guidance

1. In 2001 ULB launched a coordinating committee for both students (traditional target of pedagogical activities organized by different services) and faculty. Since 2007 *Centre des technologies au service de l'enseignement* (CTE) (created in 1999 within the department of support for academic activities) has organized initial training and provided support for educational/ICT innovation through a special unit, called PRAC-TICE. In the faculty of applied science, a pedagogical unit offers specific support to faculty on teaching innovation, evaluation, and training.

2. *Institut de formation et de recherche en enseignement supérieur* (IFRES), officially launched in January 2005, coordinates existing activities to support teaching: formal training programs (FORMASUP, CAPAES), two research support units (SMART on evaluation, LABSET on distance learning), innovative teaching in medicine, and the *Centre de didactique supérieure* (CDS).

3. *Diplôme d'études spécialisées* (DES), previously organized by UCL and ULG, became a *Master complémentaire en pédagogie universitaire et de l'enseignement supérieur* in 2007–2008.

4. *Service de pédagogie universitaire* offers support to both students and teachers.

undertake research. The units provide generic training sessions for faculty members and, sometimes, for teaching assistants. Workshops can be one-time events or can be organized as yearlong programs. These sessions focus on developing basic instructional skills, and teachers learn how to design a course, develop study materials for their students, and assess student learning. Integrating new technologies in teaching, especially the application of digital learning environments, is a major focus of these sessions. Only the unit associated with the University of Antwerp provides services to nonuniversity institutions of higher education associated with the university; the other units focus mainly on the university community.

On the whole, one can conclude that faculty development in Flemish universities—with the exception of K.U. Leuven—focuses primarily on instructional development. The unit at K.U. Leuven is also active in curriculum development and quality assurance.

In French-speaking universities, both centralized and decentralized units have a tradition of supporting students rather than academics. These units offer individual students personal advice and workshops on program and course selection, study strategies, and the like. Most universities—with the notable exception of the Université Catholique de Louvain [UCL]—lack an extended history of a centralized unit dedicated solely to faculty development.[12] Only recently have some established such a unit to coordinate existing but dispersed activities or to launch new activities (for example, Université libre de Bruxelles [ULB] and Université de Liège [ULG]). Others (for example, Université de Mons-Hainaut [UMH], Faculté polytechnique de Mons [FPMs], Facultés universitaires Saint-Louis [FuSL], and Facultés universitaires catholiques de Mons [FUCAM]) still do not have a specific unit dedicated to faculty development. One can expect, however, that this will change in the near future, since the March 2004 decree stipulates (art. 83, §1) that universities must launch a new *Centre de didactique supérieure* (CDS) in each *académie* "to give advice, training, and support to faculty teaching first-year undergraduate students." At a minimum, universities will have to collaborate in and coordinate their faculty development offerings for teachers who work with undergraduate students.

K.U. Leuven and UCL

The leaders in creating an official unit for faculty development in Belgium have been K.U. Leuven for the Flemish (1977)[13] and UCL for the French

(1995)[14] institutions. These units are of special interest because they are the oldest in the country and possess certain characteristics that help to explain Belgian higher education, in general, and faculty development, in particular.

What most distinguishes these units from other similar ones in Belgium is twofold: domains of development, and position and mission.

University-Wide Teaching Philosophy

In 1999 both K.U. Leuven and UCL adopted a university-wide teaching philosophy: guided independent learning (Elen, 2003) for the former, and *gérer sa formation* for the latter. Both conceptual approaches are open rather than prescriptive in that they do not dictate specific teaching strategies teachers must use. They seek to engage teachers in reflecting on decisions about designing and enacting their teaching in their particular context. This is not to say that neither university provides guidelines; on the contrary, both guided independent learning and *gérer sa formation* put forward basic characteristics of good teaching practices. It is not surprising that these characteristics correspond to research findings reported in the international literature in the field: student learning is and should be the central focus of attention, and students should take responsibility for their own learning. Moreover, students are expected to take an active role in learning, and in so doing, increase their autonomy and sense of control and achievement. In the process, they have to be able to count on the support of their teachers. Moreover, through research into good teaching practices, teachers can gauge the effectiveness of their own approach.

Diversity of Programs and Initiatives

K.U. Leuven and UCL offer a range of programs for teachers, as do other faculty development units. The best known are programs targeted to specific groups, such as new faculty members or teaching assistants. These initiatives are typically organized centrally. At K.U. Leuven, programs for novice teaching assistants are now offered locally within faculties, and facilitation necessitates close collaboration between central and local faculty developers.

In addition to university-wide initiatives accessible to all faculty members (even to those from other higher-education institutions with which the universities are closely collaborating), both units are responsive to specific demands. They have dedicated resources to plan, deliver, and coordinate initiatives based on specific requests from academic units; these can be for groups of teachers within a faculty or can involve coaching at the individual level. In the latter case, for instance, a teacher, together with a faculty developer associated with the central or local unit, might scrutinize the impact of the individual's teaching practices on students' learning processes. The units also provide operational and educational support for what one might call "small" action-research projects on the impact of particular teaching approaches.

Domains of Development

The units at K.U. Leuven and UCL, like those in most other Belgian universities, support instructional development and educational innovation. In the late 1990s, academic authorities at both universities created special annual funds for innovation (Frenay & Paul, 2006; Waeytens et al., 2003) distributed on a competitive basis. The two faculty development units play an important role in assisting teachers to prepare their proposals and design their projects efficiently. Even when teachers do not obtain funding, the units may use their own resources to support interesting projects. This makes it possible for teachers to build close relationships with faculty members and to be aware of their needs. It has proven to be an adequate strategy for determining which subjects are relevant for future instructional development initiatives.

The faculty development units in K.U. Leuven and UCL stand out among similar units in sister universities in the breadth of their involvement in curriculum development and quality assurance. In both cases, this involvement is supportive in nature. Neither unit evaluates or elaborates study programs as such; rather, each unit provides consultancy, advice, and operational support for curriculum (evaluation) committees working within faculties. More concretely, the units help to design and administer questionnaires and to follow up on results of evaluations and anticipate and prepare for possible consequences of curriculum changes. These kinds of development activities can—and often—have very educating effects. As such, initiatives in quality assurance, curriculum development, and educational innovation contribute to faculty members' educational professionalization, and pedagogical development depends on these domains.

Very often these types of activities lead directly to development of specific training programs. For instance, if a curriculum audit reveals that teaching quality suffers because of poor use of technology, a program committee might call on the central unit to organize training on blended learning. Also with regard to the content of instructional development initiatives, the activities of the units in other domains play a crucial and beneficial role in providing required expertise and experience. For example, research findings of a unit on innovation in digital learning environments can be used in workshops on this theme (Buelens, Totté, Deketelaere, & Dierickx, 2007). Providing quality educational development thus hinges on maintaining a close connection among all domains for which a unit is responsible as well as maintaining the flow of dialogue and intensive collaboration among team members.

Position and Structure

The traditional model for faculty development units at K.U. Leuven, UCL, and other Belgian universities has been the centralized unit. Recently, however, there has been an emerging trend toward restyling this type of organization. In line with Boud's (1999) definition of development as a multidimensional and distributed activity, educational development is no longer considered the exclusive domain or responsibility of a central educational support unit. Systematic improvement in quality of education increasingly necessitates working with groups of faculty members and teaching assistants at the department and faculty levels. Indeed, one can argue that training individual teachers is not very promising when it comes to sustainable and fundamental change (Gibbs, 1996). Massy, Wilger, and Colbeck (1994) point to two important factors that contribute to difficulties individual teachers experience when attempting to transfer what they have learned, or *a fortiori*, to influence colleagues to take part in innovation: a strong culture of academic freedom and a lack of communication about teaching (Massy et al., 1994).

In contrast to existing central and generic programs, local and very often discipline-specific initiatives are seen as more effective alternatives. Boud (1999), for instance, points out that well-designed university-wide educational development initiatives have their merits, but they generally do not have a real impact on faculty members to the extent that faculty can apply what they have learned to their own teaching environment. This does not imply that all centrally organized initiatives should be replaced by local ones, which would entail considerable risks if local initiatives were too casual, uninformed by recent research findings, and not rigorously scrutinized and evaluated. The two units referred to appear to be adhering to this advocated trend. While they offer a series of centrally organized educational development initiatives, they also invest in local initiatives. At K.U. Leuven, the creation of a local unit for educational support in each of 13 faculties in 2007 demonstrates the importance the institution places on decentralization. At UCL, local educational development initiatives[15] have become affiliated with the central unit, and they jointly organize local activities to train faculty members and teaching assistants. There is always concern about balance when combining a central program and a local one. In this regard, Hicks has argued for an integrated approach to faculty development (Hicks, 1999). This implies that the content and methods of central and local initiatives be closely aligned.

Missions

The K.U. Leuven and UCL approach to educational development is both service- and research-oriented, and this is not surprising since both are located in research-intensive universities. The credibility of programs and support offered through the faculty development unit depends heavily on a scientifically sound basis. In keeping with the notion of scholarship of teaching, both units engage in research in close collaboration with teachers. UCL initiated formal collaboration with the Department of Education by creating the UNESCO Chair of University Teaching and Learning in 2002 to advance two types of initiatives: applied research projects (for example, evaluating the problem-based learning [PBL] curriculum of engineering [Galand & Frenay, 2005] and training students pursuing a formal diploma in teaching and learning in higher education [DES][16]).

Characteristics of Instructional Development at K.U. Leuven and UCL

Instructional development initiatives at K.U. Leuven and UCL share a number of characteristics, which we describe here.

Teach What You Preach

The main goal of all instructional development initiatives is to enable teachers to implement and advance the university's teaching philosophy to improve students' learning experiences. The design of these initiatives is necessarily grounded in the assumptions of the same philosophy:

- Goals of instructional development initiatives are carefully formulated and communicated to participants who are invited to determine their own goals for specific activities (for example, long-term programs for novice faculty members and course design programs).
- The learning environment of instructional development initiatives is adjusted to characteristics of participants. Participants are invited to actively engage in instructional development initiatives through careful choices of teaching methods, materials, assignments, and intensive coaching. With long-term instructional development initiatives, participants are carefully followed up outside of group sessions.
- All instructional development initiatives are carefully evaluated.

Learning to Teach and Learning About Teaching

Instructional development initiatives discuss recent insights from educational research about teaching. Moreover, attention is devoted to specific teaching practices and the role of participants in teaching and learning events. Faculty members and teaching assistants, for instance, work on their own courses by, for example, experimenting with certain ideas in microteaching sessions and *in vivo*. Because current literature on educational research always informs the process of learning to teach, instructional development initiatives transcend the simplistic level of "tips and tricks" (McKeachie, 1996). Making the connection with published literature emphasizes that education is a subject for research, and that the results of this research can inspire one's practice. Through this approach, participants explicitly reflect on their own teaching (Korthagen, 1992).

Research-Based Focus and Promotion of Scholarship of Teaching

The teaching philosophies of guided independent learning and *gérer sa formation* both explicitly stress a teaching research nexus. The concepts state, for example, that university teaching is scientifically up-to-date. The same principle also applies to instructional development. Recent research findings are the starting point when making decisions about content and design of instructional development programs.

Educational research is the basis of instructional development in both content and form. In line with innovative ideas in the literature (Boyer, 1990; Shulman, 2003), all instructional development initiatives explicitly encourage researching one's own teaching. Participants in initiatives are researchers by definition, and they are interested in analyzing the quality and impact of their particular teaching approach. This kind of research enables them to make well-informed decisions about their teaching practices and sometimes even leads to publishing findings. From personal reports of experiences, it is clear that faculty members consider this personally interesting and professionally satisfying.

Challenges Facing Universities and Faculty Development

Overall our experience demonstrates that faculty development in Belgium is very diverse. Some institutions focus primarily on instructional development, whereas others embrace a fuller notion of educational development. Most universities, though, pay much greater attention to the quality of their teaching today than they did in the past. Yet, despite increasing attention to and growing goodwill for education, particularly at research-intensive universities, faculty development in Belgium faces serious challenges.

As we mentioned in the introduction to this chapter, universities are experiencing unprecedented pressure concerning the quality of their education—from students and society at large and from the new accreditation process resulting from the Bologna Declaration. We expect that there will be intense questioning of instructional development activities: Are they aligned sufficiently with particular needs of participants so they empower individuals to deliver high-quality education? Do they have real impact? Does participation in instructional development initiatives guarantee that quality of education will improve?

As with most faculty development units worldwide, workshops are the predominant format of initiatives. Some are part of longer trajectories that may culminate in a formal graduate diploma (for example, a Master in Higher Education). Others are one-time or involve individual coaching. As such, Belgian faculty development units do not seem to differ significantly from those in other countries. Lycke (1999), for instance, notes that workshops are still the most popular type of faculty development initiative internationally.

Notwithstanding similarities with faculty development activities in other countries, there are several unique and notable emerging trends:

- Such activities pay greater attention to individual consultation and coaching, since this type of instructional development makes it possible to respond to very particular needs.
- Faculty developers provide increased support for recipients of educational innovation grants.
- There is a tendency to offer more integrated programs (instead of isolated workshops) to increase potential impact on teaching practices.
- There are more programs for groups of faculty members from the same department to increase the potential of impact on teaching practices.

Development units at both K.U. Leuven and UCL are experimenting with these so-called new approaches to educational development. For example, they invest in departmental initiatives adjusted to the particular context and educational needs of participants, acknowledging the fact that most faculty members identify first and foremost with their own departments. Also, cross-departmental initiatives that stay close to participants' academic home are being developed. These make it possible to acknowledge both disciplinary traditions and complexities of working contexts and duties.

It may seem that these types of instructional development initiatives contribute to improving the quality of education. However, empirical data about the impact of instructional development on quality of instruction, and more important, quality of student learning, are scarce (Prebble et al., 2005). For the credibility of faculty development, it is crucial that educational developers show evidence of the impact of their work. In this respect, it is remarkable that the vast majority of faculty development units in Belgium do not invest significantly in researching the impact of their initiatives. Exceptions are evaluations of teaching innovation funds (Frenay & Paul, 2006; Waeytens et al., 2003) and nascent attempts to evaluate initial teacher training (Clement, Laga, & Buelens, 2005; Frenay, Wouters, Bourgeois, & Galand, 2005; Stes, Clement, & Van Petegem, 2007). Clearly, much more work is needed in this area.

The growing attention to quality of education has caused universities to articulate more precisely the importance of teaching and how they perceive the balance between teaching and research. To evaluate faculty members on research output only does not correspond with the growing emphasis placed on high-quality education. Consequently, universities struggle with the value they attach to teaching and the implications this may have for faculty members' careers and evaluations.

With regard to faculty development, this challenge leads specifically to whether participation in initiatives for instructional development should be mandatory. Participation in instructional development is voluntary in Belgian universities.[17] As a result, those who participate are motivated to learn, which provides a comfortable starting point for the educational developers with whom they interact. Yet, instructional development initiatives are not only for individual teachers; they can also support realization of the institution's goals (Brew & Boud, 1996). It seems obvious that a university has a right to expect each of its teachers to be familiar and comply with its teaching philosophy. The challenge is to strike a balance between the comfort zone of motivated and voluntary participants and the expectations the institution sets. Efforts to resolve the tensions between academic freedom and obligation and between individual and institutional needs imply a positive approach to educational development. Participation is positively rewarded and structurally embedded. This goes beyond the factual question of whether participation in instructional development activities should be obligatory. It suggests that the value a university attaches to educational development is clear from the measures the institution takes. For example, that both K.U. Leuven and UCL require faculty to submit a teaching dossier as part of their tenure and promotion process is a step toward creating an embedded approach, albeit only one of many they could take. The political aspect of faculty development work—for example, advocating for improved teaching and learning capacity in institutions—is an especially pertinent but potentially contentious point for Belgian faculty development units in the near future.

A third challenge facing universities is the expansion of their formal networks with other higher-education institutions. Creating collaborative networks (*associaties* and *académies*) implies that many more faculty members, with possibly greatly differing individual concerns, need to be served. For instance, the development unit at K.U. Leuven employs two permanent and two temporary full-time staff members for all central as well as local initiatives; they serve more than 2,200 faculty members and may be called on by as many faculty at the level of the *associatie*. This places a huge demand on the unit. One response to this challenge might be to invest in training new educational developers who can take charge of instructional development at the institutional level outside the university or within the university at the department level (rather than hiring more people at the central level). The EU–Canada mobility project (Frenay, Saroyan, et al., 2005) was especially interesting in this aspect, since it focused on developing curriculum for this new target group. Work still needs to be done, however, to formalize this program and its implementation in Belgian universities. This has serious implications for target groups of instructional development and for relevance of content of initiatives across the board. It also raises the question of what an appropriate profile of an educational developer will be in the future.

Conclusion

Higher education in Belgium is a dynamic field. Ongoing efforts of all higher-education institutions to cope with the consequences of the Bologna Declaration, to a large extent, speak to the turbulent climate. Existing and expanding units of faculty development are of great help in responding to these challenges. Indeed, most higher-education institutions have a faculty development unit geared toward a specified teaching philosophy that provides a diverse set of initiatives on instructional development; educational innovation; and, sometimes, curriculum development and quality assurance. Consequently, one could argue that most Belgian higher-education institutions seem to be aware of the need to invest in faculty development to deliver high-quality teaching. Yet, some challenges remain in the short term, including responsiveness to demands for accountability, finding the balance between teaching and research, and growth of collaborative networks that introduce new issues to those managing existing faculty development resources. These challenges raise issues for faculty development units, especially concerning types of initiatives and their impact, the nature of participation and target groups, and content of programs. No doubt, these factors will oblige faculty development units in the future to assume a more assertive political role of advocating for improved teaching and learning capacity in their institutions and for resources that will enable them to carry out a broader mandate.

Notes

1. *Hautes écoles* or *hogescholen* are higher-education institutions that are not universities. They closely approximate technical/vocational postsecondary institutions.

2. Level 5 refers to the first stage of tertiary education (not leading directly to an advanced research qualification).

3. Level 6 stands for the second stage of tertiary education (leading to an advanced research qualification).

4. In 2005 the pass rate at U.C. Louvain was 48%. In 2006 the success rate for first-year undergraduates at K.U. Leuven was 51%.

5. The academic duties of this group are defined in terms of teaching, research, and service to the community, with a maximum teaching load of 50%.

6. Part-time teachers hold a PhD degree but are given only teaching duties, and their appointment may be sessional. Their teaching load varies according to the number of courses for which they are appointed.

7. Researchers hold a PhD degree and are hired by the French- or Flemish-speaking funds for research: *Fonds de recherche scientifique* (FRS) or *Funds voor wettenschapelijk onderzoek* (FWO). They may teach up to two courses per year.

8. The European Credit Transfer and Accumulation System (ECTS) is a student-centered system based on the workload required to achieve the objectives of a program—objectives preferably specified in terms of learning outcomes and competences to be acquired. Introduced in 1989 within the framework of Erasmus, and now part of the Socrates program, ECTS is the only credit system that has been successfully tested and used across Europe. ECTS was set up initially for credit transfers. The system facilitated recognizing periods of study abroad and thus enhanced the quality and volume of student mobility in Europe. Recently ECTS also began developing into an accumulation system to be implemented at institutional, regional, national, and European levels—one of the key objectives of the Bologna Declaration.

9. The five *associaties* are Association K.U. Leuven: K.U. Leuven University and 12 *hogescholen*; Association University–Hogescholen Limburg: Transnational University Limburg and two *hogescholen*; Association University of Ghent: University of Ghent and three *hogescholen*; Association University and Hogescholen Antwerp: University of Antwerp and four *hogescholen*; and Association Brussels: University of Brussels and one *hogescholen*.

10. These are Académie Louvain: Université catholique de Louvain (UCL), Facultés universitaires catholiques de Mons (FUCAM), Facultés universitaires Saint-Louis (FUSL), and Facultés universitaires Notre-Dame de la Paix (FUNDP); Académie Wallonie-Bruxelles: Université de Mons-Hainaut (UMH), Faculté polytechnique de Mons (FPMs), and Université libre de Bruxelles (ULB); and Académie Wallonie-Europe: Université de Liège (ULG) and Faculté de sciences appliquées de Gembloux (FSAGx).

11. We systematically analyzed the Web sites of these universities to extract this information in July 2007.

12. In 1987 FuNDP began an internal newsletter (*réseau*) that offers faculty an opportunity to reflect on their teaching within their *Service de pédagogie universitaire*; since 1985 this has focused mainly on offering support to students on learning and study strategies.

13. *Dienst Universitaire Onderwijs* (DUO).

14. *Institut de pédagogie universitaire et des multimédias* (IPM).

15. This trend is likely to continue into the near future, since the university administration has planned to have three decentralized units of educational development: one for the medical sector, one for the sciences sector, and one for the human and social sciences sector.

16. The DES, launched in 2002, became a specialized Master in Higher Education as of 2008–2009.

17. A notable exception is the University of Liège. Since July 2007, new faculty are obliged to attend compulsory training (five days within two years) coordinated centrally by the *Institut de formation et de recherche en enseignement supérieur* (IFRES).

References

Bologna Declaration. (1999). *Joint declaration of the European Ministers of Education convened in Bologna on the 19th of June 1999*. Retrieved from http://ec.europa.eu/education/policies/educ/bologna/bologna.pdf.

Boud, D. (1999). Situating academic development in professional work: Using peer learning. *The International Journal for Academic Development, 4*(1), 3–10.

Boyer, E. L. (1990). *Scholarship reconsidered: Priorities of the professoriate*. Princeton, NJ: The Carnegie Foundation for the Advancement of Teaching.

Brew, A., & Boud, D. (1996). Preparing for new academic roles: An holistic approach to development. *The International Journal for Academic Development, 1*(2), 17–25.

Buelens, H., Totté, N., Deketelaere, A., & Dierickx, K. (2007). Electronic discussion forums in medical education: The Impact of didactical guidelines and etiquette. *Medical Education, 41*(7), 711–717.

Clement, M., Laga, E., & Buelens, H. (2005, April). *Evaluation of a TA training program in a Flemish university: Findings and challenges*. Paper presented at the annual meeting of the American Educational Research Association, Montreal, Canada.

Clement, M., McAlpine, L., & Waeytens, K. (2004). Fascinating Bologna: Impact on the nature and approach of academic development. *The International Journal for Academic Development, 9*(2), 127–131.

Elen, J. (2003). Reality of excellence in higher education: The case of guided independent learning at the Katholieke Universiteit Leuven. In E. De Corte (Ed.), *Excellence in higher education* (pp. 109–126). London: Portland Press.

Eurostat. (2005). *Europe in figures: Eurostat yearbook 2005.* Retrieved from http://epp.eurostat.ec.europa.eu/cache/ITY_OFFPUB/KS-CD-05-001/EN/KS-CD-05-001-EN.PDF.

Frenay, M., & Paul, C. (2006). Le développement de projets pédagogiques: Reflet ou source de l'engagement de l'enseignant universitaire dans ses activités d'enseignement? [Developing educational projects: Reflection or source for the engagement of faculty in their teaching duties?]. In N. Rege Colet & M. Romainville (Eds.), *La pratique enseignante en mutation à l'université* [Change of teaching practice in universities] (pp. 103–128). Bruxelles, Belgium: De Boeck.

Frenay, M., Saroyan, A., Clement, M., Kolmos, A., Paul, J.-J., Bédard, D., Taylor, L., & Rege Colet, N. (2005). *FACDEV program: Promoting faculty development to enhance the quality of learning in higher education.* Bruxelles, Belgium: European Union, DG Education and Culture.

Frenay, M., Wouters, P., Bourgeois, E., & Galand, B. (2005, April). *Evaluation of a teacher program in a French-Belgian university: The use of teaching portfolios.* Paper presented at the annual meeting of the American Educational Research Association, Montréal, Canada.

Galand, B., & Frenay, M. (2005). *L'approche par projets et par problèmes dans l'enseignement supérieur: Impact, enjeux et défis* [Project and problem-based approaches in higher education: Impact, issues and challenges]. Louvain-la-Neuve, Belgium: Presses Universitaires de Louvain.

Gibbs, G. (1996). Supporting educational development within departments. *The International Journal for Academic Development, 6*(1), 27–37.

Hicks, O. (1999). Integration of central and departmental development: Reflections from Australian universities. *The International Journal for Academic Development, 4*(1), 43–51.

Korthagen, F. A. J. (1992). Techniques for stimulating reflection in teacher education seminars. *Teaching and Teacher Education, 8*(3), 265–274.

Lycke, K. H. (1999). Faculty development: Experiences and issues in a Norwegian perspective. *The International Journal for Academic Development, 4*(2), 124–133.

Massy, W. F., Wilger, A. K., & Colbeck, C. (1994). Departmental cultures and teaching quality: Overcoming "hollowed" collegiality. *Change, 26*(4), 11–20.

McKeachie, W. J. (1996, June). *Critical elements in training university teachers.* Paper presented at the 1st International Consortium for Educational Development Conference, Vasa, Finland.

Prebble, T., Hargraves, H., Leach, L., Naidoo, K., Suddaby, G., & Zepke, N. (2005). *Impact of student support services and academic development programmes on student outcomes in undergraduate tertiary study: A synthesis of the research.* Retrieved from http://www.educationcounts.govt.nz/publications/tertiary_education/5519.

Shulman, L. S. (2003). Scholarship of teaching in higher education. In E. De Corte (Ed.), *Excellence in higher education* (pp. 73–82). London: Portland.

Stes, A., Clement, M., & Van Petegem, P. (2007). The effectiveness of a faculty training program: Long term and institutional impact. *The International Journal for Academic Development, 12*(2), 99–109.

Verhesschen, P., & Verburgh, A. (2004). The introduction of the bachelor-master's structure at the K.U. Leuven: Challenges and opportunities for faculty development. *The International Journal for Academic Development, 9*(2), 133–152.

Waeytens, K., Elen, J., Billiet, J., Debrock, M., Driesen, J., Halsberghe, E., & Willems, P. (2003). Onderwijsinnovatie: Loont het de moeite? [Educational innovation: Rewards worth the trouble?]. In N. Druine, M. Clement, & K. Waeytens (Eds.), *Dynamiek in het hoger onderwijs. Uitdagingen voor onderwijsondersteuning* [Dynamics in the higher education. Challenges for educational development] (pp. 179–191). Leuven, Belgium: Universitaire Pers Leuven.

5

A LOOK AT THE FRENCH
EXPERIENCE IN FACULTY
DEVELOPMENT

Jean-Jacques Paul and Noël Adangnikou
Translation by Julie Timmermans

T he extent of faculty development activities in the four countries
described in the preceding chapters might make the French academic who is open to the idea of pedagogical training, and who
considers teaching as more than an art, quite envious. Faculty development
activities are not a primary concern in the French context. The rare initiatives that do exist are few and far between, and many academics continue to
perceive the very notion of university teaching negatively.

Why does France differ so markedly from other countries in this regard?
Why do French universities remain on the sidelines of changes that a univer-
sity such as Harvard intends to promote (see "Harvard Task Force," 2007)?
What emerging developments might foreshadow a new landscape?

Structure and Regulations

Perhaps the leading reason for the indifference toward teaching in France is
that, from the selection and hiring process of new faculty to the evaluation
methods used during an academic's entire career, the sole factor considered
is research productivity.

Recruitment in France occurs at both the national and local levels. To
apply for a position as an associate professor (or a professor), a candidate

must first be qualified by the *Conseil national des universités* (National University Counsel), a body made up of elected and appointed disciplinary faculty comprising 74 departments or disciplinary areas. While the *Conseil* provides specific requirements that it defines and publishes nationally, universities are ultimately responsible for actual recruiting. At the time of hiring, experience as a teaching assistant or other teaching may be an advantage for a young candidate, but it is never a requirement. Contrary to the practice in Sweden, Norway, and Denmark, there is no formal requirement for university teachers to obtain pedagogical qualifications. The expectations are somewhat different for doctoral students who take on teaching assistantships during their studies. They are required to take 10 days of seminars annually at one of the 14 *Centres d'initiation à l'enseignement supérieur* (CIES) (Centers for Introduction to Teaching in Higher Education). According to teaching assistants, however, these seminars seem to lack coherence and relevance to university teaching. This criticism is likely due to the sparse resources allocated to CIES (Coulon, Ennafaa, & Paivandi, 2003; Dejean, 2002), and to the dearth of available experts in university teaching. Bireaud's (1996) observation regarding students' disinterest in these training sessions may also have some merit. She asserts that PhD students give priority to their research and dissertation, as hiring decisions are based primarily on the quality and outcome of these. On average, 10% of doctoral students participate in these seminars, and of these, about half end up being the new cohort of associate professors.

Another important characteristic of the French system is that a candidate who is successful is hired directly into a tenured position, not into a temporary position subject to review. In fact, even though there is a two-year probationary period, tenure is granted in almost all cases, because the tenure decision is based primarily on meeting specific bureaucratic standards (for example, number of required course-hours completed), not on the content and quality of the individual's instruction.

Using evidence of teaching performance, such as teaching portfolios, or student course ratings as we might see in Canada, for example, remains inconceivable for the moment when research is the only criterion for promotion, and regular evaluation of teaching activities is nonexistent. The only mandatory instances of evaluation are those tied to a request for promotion. In other words, a faculty member who never requests a promotion will never be evaluated formally. And when an individual applies for promotion, the request generally becomes competitive in nature. In this context, any effort the candidate might have made in pedagogical innovations would not be as valued as would a research paper published in a scholarly journal. In other words, unlike Canada, where the system offers extrinsic motivation to encourage individuals to participate in teaching development activities, or Belgian universities (for example, Louvain and Leuven), which encourage their instructors' pedagogical development and take these efforts into account in promotion policies, the system in France is indifferent to teaching development. Indeed, taking into account teaching accomplishments in promotion policies would be an anomaly in France.

Yet another feature the countries represented in the four previous chapters stress is evaluation of teaching and its consequences on a faculty member's career. Although teaching evaluations theoretically have been mandatory since 1997,[1] the university community in France is nowhere close to Canadian universities, where 94% report using student evaluations of instruction. French higher-education institutions see resistance to any form of evaluation as necessary to avoid any potential infringement on the principle of academic freedom granted to guarantee a faculty[2] member's autonomy in course design. This illustrates the discrepancy between what is recommended at the national level and what the actual practice is at the institutional level. Even when evaluations are conducted, they are not disseminated at the departmental or faculty levels. The intended audience is the faculty member, department chair, and the dean of the faculty, but an evaluation may not be linked to a faculty member's career. As an illustration of what was mentioned earlier, the *Conseil des études et de la vie universitaire* (CEVU), whose mandate includes examining proposals to maintain existing degrees or create new degrees, does not consider evaluations in their overall assessment.

Within the French landscape of faculty development, a few faculty development centers are associated with universities. As of 2005, there were about 20 of these centers among 88 universities. The absence of either initial or ongoing training for the profession of faculty developer is evident, and faculty developers who practice in these centers are not considered to be professionals. In this climate, it is rare for a university to dedicate resources to training and remunerating administrative personnel who devote part or all of their time to faculty development.

Institutional Context and Epistemology

The institutional context that stems from the specific position of the French universities within the larger higher-education system and the epistemological context related to educational research may also help to explain the general disregard for teaching and faculty development. Universities have never been a political or financial priority in France because training the elite falls to the *grandes écoles* (prestigious higher-education institutions with competitive entrance examinations) and, before them, to the *classes préparatoires* (programs that prepare students for entrance examinations to *grandes écoles*). Admission to these programs is extremely selective, and training is based on a high level of supervision and traditional pedagogical methods. Mass higher education is left to the university, and instruction consists, by and large, of lecturing in amphitheaters to large audiences. These *ex cathedra* lectures might be accompanied by tutorials or labs with fewer students. Tutorials are generally devoted to group work and marking exercises that have been distributed beforehand. Labs are an opportunity to practice applied skills (for example, foreign languages, computing). While this rather conservative instructional model is quite the norm, it has not precluded pedagogical innovations, albeit marginal, in e-learning and project- or problem-based learning (PBL).

It is worth noting that the total spending per *university* student is markedly lower in France than in the other countries discussed in this volume. Total spending per university student in France is $8,600; it is $11,842 in Belgium, $15,225 in Denmark, and $21,366 in Switzerland (Organisation for Economic Co-operation and Development [OECD], 2005).[3] Total spending per student by *classes préparatoires* or by engineering schools represents double the amount that is spent per university student, so it is not hard to imagine why funding for pedagogical innovation in France is likely to be limited.

Most teachers and researchers in France pay little attention to university pedagogy because of the low esteem in general for the discipline of education. This discipline is often considered too heterogeneous, without a unified method, and closer to discourse and rhetoric than to science. In this context, research on university teaching and learning is sparse and undervalued, and as a consequence, it is difficult for the community of researchers in university teaching and learning to establish themselves and gain any recognition (Adangnikou, 2008).

Prospects for the Future

In light of all of this, must we expect that faculty development experiences in the other four countries discussed in this book will never apply to France? The outlook need not be so pessimistic as some factors in the current context have the potential to highlight the importance of university teaching and training of university teachers. One such factor is the decrease in the number of university students, particularly in certain scientific programs, which might lead to considering changes in instructional methods to make such programs more attractive. Furthermore, the Ministry of Higher Education is becoming increasingly demanding regarding evaluation, though at present, it stops short of expecting faculty teaching to be evaluated.

Another factor that might inspire change regarding pedagogical approaches and the competencies required to implement them is the increase in competition among universities tied to the Bologna process. With the August 2007 law on autonomy of French universities, and the expansion and change in the composition of the boards of governors, one could foresee that external members would have fewer qualms about raising the issue of teaching quality and instructors' pedagogical competencies.

Institutional attempts to set up university teaching centers may also spread, even though the 20 or so existing centers remain very dependent on local (that is, the university's) political power. One illustration of this is the center at Université de Bourgogne, which owes its existence to the initiative of a vice president who was a member of the Faculty Development Student Mobility Project that was the genesis of this book. Despite the success in establishing this center, its survival remains tenuous, particularly as budgetary constraints become more acute.

A final promising initiative that might further strengthen the nascent faculty development movement in France is a network, entitled *Réseau des structures universitaires de pédagogie* (RSUP) (Network of University Structures for Pedagogy), established in 2005 by six faculty development centers. This network seeks to enable its members to share experiences; work closely; and, by its strength as a group, promote and influence faculty development (RSUP, 2006). But like development centers themselves, this network is nascent and vulnerable to external pressures. The anticipated renewal of faculty to address needs caused by increasing student enrollments and the consolidation of European higher education emphasized by the Bologna process—

which promotes an increase in student and faculty mobility, a means of strengthening both collaboration and competition among universities—may create an environment in which faculty development practices take on new significance. In this scenario, the examples of the other countries shared in this volume provide a road map to negotiate the complex issues inherent in entrenching robust faculty development practices within France's university community.

Notes

1. Order from the Minister of National Education, F. Bayrou, April 9, 1997, articles 23 & 24.

2. In the French universities, the associate professors and professors are called *enseignants-chercheurs*, which explicitly refers to the two missions of universities: research and teaching. In this chapter, we refer to them as faculty.

3. For Canada, 2003 figures indicate an average per student expenditure of $19,992 for tertiary education (OECD, 2006).

References

Adangnikou, N. (2008). Peut-on parler de recherche en pédagogie universitaire aujourd'hui en France? [Can we talk of research on university teaching today in France?]. *Revue des sciences de l'éducation, 34*(3), 601–621.

Bireaud, A. (1996). En France, une politique de formation pédagogique pour les enseignants du supérieur timide, hésitante et controversée [In France, a shy, hesitating and controversial policy for the pedagogical development of higher education teachers]. In J. Donnay & M. Romainville (Eds.), *Enseigner à l'université, un métier qui s'apprend?* [To teach in universities: A profession to learn?] (pp. 113–122). Bruxelles, Belgium: De Boeck.

Coulon, A., Ennafaa, R., & Paivandi, S. (2003). *Les allocataires moniteurs de l'enseignement supérieur* [The teaching assistants in higher education] (Vol. 03.10). Paris: Centre de recherches sur l'enseignement supérieur (ESCOL).

Dejean, J. (2002). *L'évaluation de l'enseignement dans les universités françaises* [The evaluation of teaching in French universities]. Paris: Haut Conseil pour l'évaluation de l'école.

Harvard task force calls for new focus on teaching and not just research. (2007, May 10). *New York Times*. Retrieved from http://www.nytimes.com/2007/05/10/education/10harvard.html.

Organisation for Economic Co-operation and Development (OECD) (Ed.). (2005). *OECD in figures*. Paris: Author.

Organisation for Economic Co-operation and Development (OECD). (2006). *Education at a glance—OECD indicators*. Paris: Author.

Réseau des structures universitaires de pédagogie (RSUP). (2006, May). *La formation pédagogique des enseignants du supérieur dans le réseau des SUP en France* [The instructional development of faculty in the SUP network in France]. Paper presented at the 23rd Conference of the Association internationale de pédagogie universitaire [International Association on University Teaching and Learning], Monastir, Tunisie.

6

FACULTY DEVELOPMENT ACROSS EUROPE AND CANADA

Comparisons of Five Case Studies

Mariane Frenay and Alenoush Saroyan

U niversities today face challenges that have unequivocal implications for faculty development initiatives. The pressure to offer high-quality education, questions about the value of teaching compared with that of research, and the new landscape of higher-education institutions, especially in the context of Bologna process implementation, imply that educational developers in general and faculty developers in particular face new and perhaps different questions about the nature of participation, the types of initiatives offered, and the impact and accountability of faculty and educational development work on target groups.

Faculty development as a field of practice in Europe and Canada is very diverse and is shaped by national and institutional contexts and respective cultures. This observation is strongly shared by colleagues from eight universities (five in Europe, three in Canada) involved in a mobility project whose primary aim was to develop a curriculum to train faculty developers (Frenay et al., 2005). An important by-product of this mobility project was that members of this network were able to develop a better understanding of the national context of each participating country and the way in which faculty development practices have evolved within each specific context. Five national case studies (Canada, Switzerland, Denmark, Belgium, and France) presented in this book provided the input data for an in-depth perspective on practices in the respective countries. Results of a comparative analysis of experiences in these countries comprise the core of this chapter.

Current Events Leading to Faculty Development

Comparisons of the five cases representing Canada, Switzerland, Denmark, Belgium, and France bring to the fore a number of internal and external forces that have forced universities in these countries in particular, but also more generally in Europe,[1] to implement some type of faculty development activity.

In the European context, the development of some of these initiatives can be traced to global trends such as changing student demographics (for example, increase in enrollments, greater diversity), development of technologies and e-learning, challenges to funding and resources, increasing student evaluation of teaching, and educational innovation (Eurydice, 2000; Global University Network on Innovation [GUNI], 2006). Other developments are the result of recent local or regional initiatives such as the Bologna process in Europe, competition among institutions in general and ranking of universities in particular (Salmi & Saroyan, 2007), quality assurance and accreditation processes, and academic faculty renewal (Bourgeois, 2002; GUNI, 2007).

Similar to the United States, the faculty development movement in Canada was a reaction to student protests in the late 1960s and the '70s that were precipitated by dissatisfaction with the quality of teaching of subject matter experts and the uninspiring teaching methods they used (Gaff & Simpson, 1994). North American universities and colleges reacted by establishing programs and units dedicated to enhancing teaching. In Canada, the first such unit was the Centre for Learning Development, established at McGill University in 1969. Today almost all of Canada's 93 universities have dedicated units and staff engaged in faculty development.

Since the European ministers of education signed the Bologna Declaration (1999), European higher education as a whole has engaged in a large-scale restructuring process (Eurydice, 2007) with far-reaching impact (Clement, McAlpine, & Waeytens, 2004; Verhesschen & Verburgh, 2004) on both individual- and institution-level programs. For instance, higher-education institutions of 46 countries in Europe have been and are still redesigning their curricula to reach the objectives of the Bologna Declaration, operationalized through a work program that receives directions from biannual ministerial conferences. A concrete outcome of these changes is new local and national educational laws and regulations pertaining to the structure of higher education that have changed the diploma structure. What used to be certificates have now been replaced by bachelor and master degree programs (obtained after 180 and 120 additional ECTS[2] credits, respectively). More important, the ambition to have a European presence and voice in quality assurance circles has resulted in the creation of a European Association for Quality Assurance in Higher Education (ENQA). This body received a double mandate following a 2003 ministerial meeting in Berlin to explore ways of ensuring an adequate peer review system for higher-education institutions' quality assurance agencies and to develop a set of standards, procedures, and guidelines to inform internal and external review processes.[3] The quality assurance process, although still in its first phase of implementation, is exerting great pressure on institutions involved in curricular changes as a means of enhancing the quality of their education. The call for innovation and integration of technology in higher education during this process is too loud to be ignored. It is in this context that faculty development is becoming a more visible and valued activity.

National contexts and the position of higher-education systems within them are of central importance to understanding the diversity of faculty development practices in universities—from addressing national requirements for pedagogical training of faculty or doctoral students (as in Denmark and France) to an entirely voluntary process of professional development with a focus on teaching (as in Canada, Switzerland, and Belgium). In the latter set of countries, professional societies and networks of faculty developers have played an important role in developing the practice and research in the field.

To conduct the comparative analysis of the five countries involved in the Mobility Project, we used the typology offered originally by Hollingsworth and Boyer (1997) and later adapted for education systems by Dupriez and Maroy (2003; Maroy & Dupriez, 2000). This typology is depicted in Figure 6.1.[4]

The value of this model is in its capacity to delineate relationships and variations in forms of coordination. "The vertical axis refers to motives for action, but distinguishes between contexts of action motivated by self-interest alone, and those which involve more than a cost-benefit analysis—that have more to do with social norms or obligations a given actor acknowledges" (Dupriez & Maroy, 2003, p. 379). The horizontal axis captures

FIGURE 6.1
Different Forms of Coordination*

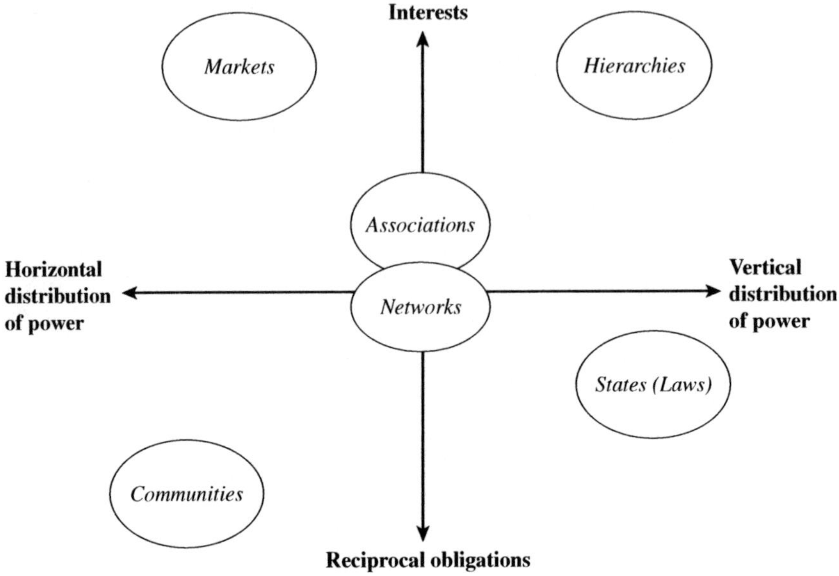

*Adapted from Maroy & Dupriez, 2000.

"modes of coordination and the distribution of power, horizontal or vertical" (p. 380). Dupriez and Maroy elaborate on this in Hollingsworth and Boyer's (1997) words to describe a continuum, one end of which depicts equal agency, whereas the other end portrays unequal agency, resulting in some hierarchical relationship (leader to follower, for example). Applying this framework to our analysis is helpful because it highlights the different regulatory bodies that exert influence on higher-education systems, and ways in which this may subsequently influence the organizational structure and development of faculty development units.

In addition to highlighting powerful modes of regulation, the model points out differences among the five countries under scrutiny here and provides insight into how these modes can affect the future of faculty development. Table 6.1 illustrates what specifically happens in each country in terms of the evolving impact of each form of coordination.

In Belgium, the following trends can be observed:

- an increase in state power and more frequent recourse to laws as a form of coordination;

TABLE 6.1
Comparison of Forms of Coordination Among Case Studies

Form of Coordination	Belgium	Canada	Denmark	France	Switzerland
Markets	Quasi-market: strong competition among universities to attract Belgian and international students (competition within Bologna process)	Quasi-market: competition among universities to attract students and faculty provincially, nationally, and internationally	Private funding, management structure, employability, accountability. Importance of attractiveness to international students	Emerging; competition among universities to attract national students; social pressure regarding high dropout rates	Quasi-market: competition among higher education institutions within dual-track system
Hierarchies (university organizations)	Reduction of "traditional" universities' autonomy (laws and regulations); autonomy regarding faculty development initiatives	Reduction of autonomy (accountability procedures); autonomy regarding faculty development initiatives	Specific training policies: relative autonomy regarding faculty development initiatives	Increase in autonomy; university initiatives regarding faculty development units	Redefinition of "research" and "professional" universities; autonomy regarding faculty development initiatives
States	Increased power of state within linguistic communities through laws and regulations in traditionally decentralized system; no federal coordination	Provincial laws and regulations (decentralized provincial system); no federal coordination, but federal incentives	Centralized system: national laws and regulations; mandatory training for new faculty	Strong centralized system: some deconcentration and/or decentralization processes	Increase in federal coordination and reduction of cantonal autonomy

TABLE 6.1 (Continued)

Form of Coordination	Belgium	Canada	Country Denmark	France	Switzerland
Associations	Consolidation of formal associations among universities—for example, *académies*	National and provincial academic associations of universities and colleges—for example, AUCC, CREPUQ			Cooperation and coordination of universities: CUS, CRUS
Networks	Formal collaboration among universities and higher education institutions outside universities—for example, *associaties*				
Communities	Some networks of professionals: French section of AIPU, Contact Research Group	Rise of educational development as profession—for example, EDC, CSSHE, STLHE	Strong national networks of faculty developers: DUN, IPN, DCN	Emerging network of SUP (since 2006)	Network of educational developers: *Réseau CFE*

- a concurrent movement toward consolidation among associations or networks of higher-education institutions;
- various developments in defining academic freedom (rise of the market); and
- a rise in forms of cooperation.

In the federal system of Belgium, laws and regulations are defined by language and cultural communities, so there is no legislated mechanism for national coordination. In recent years, however, community-level changes have affected the autonomy traditionally associated with universities. In the French-speaking community, the state is exerting a strong influence on the structure of the higher-education system in the same manner that it is influencing compulsory education (that is, primary and secondary). By redefining modes of funding, the state is imposing constraints on universities to comply with formal rules at some level, thus jeopardizing the great decision-making autonomy that institutions have enjoyed. In the context of the Bologna process, the creation of three *académies* (defined by law) in the French-speaking community could be considered a trial to initiate new forms of cooperation among universities, even though the *académies* do not supersede the traditional confessional versus non-confessional division of society and the educational system. With regard to teaching policies, the French-speaking community has pressed universities for collaboration within an *académie* to benefit undergraduates (especially first-year students). A decree of the Flemish community (that is, government) regarding universities encourages the creation of *associaties* among universities and higher-education institutions outside universities. In the typology of Hollingsworth and Boyer (1997), these would be equivalent to networks because they imply regulation and collaboration among entities that have complementary goals. So the rise in forms of cooperation among higher-education institutions in this context has taken the form of complementarity between the two types of higher-education institutions (universities and *hogescholen*). In the French-speaking higher-education context, this cooperation is left to the volition of the institutions, but the importance of the ability to attract students is one factor that leads institutions to opt in rather than out.

In Canada, the following trends can be observed:

- a rise in communities of professionals and their influence in shaping the ethos of higher education and faculty development nationally;
- increased power of the state through provincial laws and regulations;[5]
- a rise in the market as a form of coordination that implies that each university remains autonomous and defends its interests against the other institutions, including within universities; and
- reduced university autonomy with an increase in accountability procedures.

Canadian universities' high level of autonomy results in different levels of investment in faculty development units and services, which in some universities dates back three or four decades. The establishment of these units has always been a decision made at the institutional level. While they originated in response to a wave of student dissatisfaction, most units today have also assumed a proactive developmental role in their mandate. Faculty and educational developer networks are strong nationally (for example, the Educational Developers' Caucus [EDC], the Society for Teaching and Learning in Higher Education [STLHE], the Canadian Society for the Study of Higher Education [CSSHE]) and are closely linked with their U.S. (for example, the Professional and Organizational Development Network [POD]) and international counterparts. This collaboration has led to sharing of best practices—for example, the Course Design and Teaching Workshop initiated by McGill University (Saroyan & Amundsen, 2004), which 10 Canadian universities have adopted—and promotion of teaching and learning in disciplines (for example, through the STLHE annual conference and its National 3M teaching award). In the absence of a federal authority, national academic organizations (for example, the Association of Universities and Colleges of Canada [AUCC] and the Canadian Association for University Teachers [CAUT]) also undertake strong advocacy and coordination roles at the national level with respect to the higher-education development. The provincial governments have not traditionally exercised direct control over university governance, but through their funding authority, they are beginning to have a greater influence in the day-to-day operations of institutions. There is, however, some evidence that this might change.[6] Similarly, through its research funding, the federal government plays an indirect role in influencing institutional policies. For instance, with the introduction of the Canada Research Chairs Program (CRC),[7] new academic positions are created in universities in proportion to their research yield. While this has been positive for Canadian universities, it has also resulted in inequitable practices within institutions with regard to salaries and disciplines allocated to CRC positions.

Canadian institutions receive a good portion of their operational funding from their respective provincial governments; however, this funding is not at the same level across the board. Recently the provinces of Alberta and Ontario, for instance, announced significant investments in their universities and have thus become capable of more aggressive recruitment of both students and faculty. While different restrictions are placed on institutions within a given jurisdiction (for example, a freeze in Quebec university tuition fees since 1994 thawed slightly recently to allow institutions to charge students $100 more per year), institutional outcomes and ouputs measured in different ways still have direct and indirect consequences in resources gained. Annual university rankings done both nationally and internationally (Salmi & Saroyan, 2007) and institutional success in obtaining funds (by faculty and graduate students) from federal granting councils (which has implications for the number of CRCs and scholarships allocated to the institution) are examples of factors that engender fierce competition among universities.

Universities in Canada are accountable to a provincial body, typically comprising the conference of rectors/principals/presidents. In Quebec, this authority is the *Conférence des recteurs et des principaux du Québec*, which authorizes new degree programs and receives reports of cyclical programs and reviews, including self-studies and external peer reviews organized by the institutions. Professional associations independent of academe play a very important role in licensing and accrediting both individual practitioners and programs (for example, the Institute of Electrical and Electronics Engineers, Inc. for engineering and the American Psychological Association for psychology and related fields). With respect to governance, however, there are indications that provincial governments will assert a more direct presence in accountability.[8]

In Denmark, the following trends can be observed:

- the state is the main influence that regulates the university system through implementation of laws and regulations (for example, mandatory training of new faculty and the process of appointing university management);

- a rise in the market within the Bologna context (for example, pressure for greater accountability, employability, and private funding and the process of appointing academic leaders at various levels);
- maintenance of specific policies within universities concerning the organization of pedagogical training and faculty development units; and
- establishment of national networks of faculty developers and networks on university pedagogy.

Since the late 1990s, for instance, there has been a steady stream of emerging national professional networks of academic developers, such as the Danish Network for University Pedagogy (DUN), the National Pedagogical Network for Engineering Education (IPN), and the Centre for Educational Development in University Science (DCN). These national networks are essential to the vitality of faculty development initiatives in the Danish context.

Three principal trends may be highlighted in France:

- the main influence continuing to be the state, which organizes common and durable services and initiatives at universities through a centralized resource allocation system and implementation of laws and regulations;
- a recent rise in the market within the Bologna context, and with an increase in undergraduate enrollment (in particular, at universities with a science orientation[9] and in social science bachelor degrees), increasing pressure from stakeholders for accountability;[10] and
- local university initiatives to set up faculty development units at their own cost, not so much as an institutional agenda but due primarily to enthusiasm of individuals and groups concerned about the quality of teaching who consider educational development as a way to enhance it.

Finally, in Switzerland, the following trends can be highlighted:

- a rise in associations (for example, the Swiss University Conference [CUS] and the Rectors' Conference of the Swiss Universities [CRUS]) that act as quasi-coordinating bodies for all higher-education institutions located in different cantons. These bodies are concerned about

promoting and coordinating higher-education policy, and they deal
with implementation of reforms and issues, such as curriculum, syllabus, and uniformity in conditions of admission to universities;
- an increase in federal administration of the higher-education system
  facilitated by federal frameworks and corresponding bodies such as
  the Swiss University Conference (CUS), and a decrease in autonomy
  of the cantons in the administration of higher-education institutions
  located within their jurisdiction;
- a rise in the market through increased competition to attract students
  and to raise research funding of research-based universities as well as
  newly founded universities of applied sciences; and
- a need for organizations (research-led universities, referred to as hierarchies in Hollingsworth and Boyer's typology) to think about their
  identity and to state their mission of research-based teaching.

The first column in Table 6.1 provides a description of current forms of
coordination that influence higher-education systems within each country
and, by extension, university faculty development policies and practices. The
other columns help to compare the main trends and potential influences of
each form of coordination among countries.

Figure 6.2 illustrates this in a different way by presenting each specific
form of coordination and the way it influences the five countries relative to
one another. Within each sphere, the order in which the countries appear is
important; it reflects the relative influence of the specific form of coordination within the countries. So, for instance, markets and hierarchies are less
powerful for France, which has a centralized system, than they are for the
other countries. The state is much more influential in France and Denmark
than it is in Canada, Belgium, and Switzerland, which are federations with
decentralized educational systems. Associations are mainly influential in Belgium and Switzerland, and examples are the recent trend to enforce federal
coordination of Swiss universities and increased cooperation among dual-
track institutions of higher education in Belgium. Networks are specific to
Belgium and the French-speaking community where *académies* can be
found. Finally, Canada and Denmark have strong professional and academic
societies (communities in the Hollingsworth and Boyer typology) that are
capable of wielding influence on faculty development practices. This is also
somewhat the case in Switzerland and Belgium, whereas such societies are
almost nonexistent in France.

FIGURE 6.2
Influencing Forms of Coordination Among Case Studies

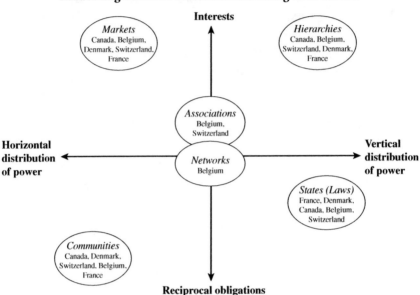

The Actual Landscape of Faculty Development

In the previous section, we highlighted current events that are creating the need for faculty development practices and supporting policies in various national and institutional contexts. While most of these events are global and affect countries in the same way, faculty development is not implemented in the same way among countries or even within a specific country. This is evident from earlier discussions and from the accounts of the five case studies. To have a better overview of the actual policies and practices of faculty development, one place to start would be to describe faculty development units within universities and their respective structures. These structures may be described by their organizational positioning within the university (line of reporting); institutional mandates and domains of activity; target audiences for their services; and educational development roles and strategies.

Table 6.2 provides a schematic perspective of the main characteristics of faculty development units in the case study countries. It provides an overview of each country's specific characteristics, but more important, it furnishes a lens for observing similarities and differences among these countries'

TABLE 6.2
A Comparison of Faculty Development Units

	Organizational Structure	Institutional Mandates and Domains of Activity	Targeted Audience	Faculty Development Roles and Strategies
Belgium	• Mostly centralized units; some partnerships with more locally situated academic units (service and research) • Discipline-specific educational development units in medicine and/or engineering	• Building learning and teaching capacity: —initial and continuing training —consulting —supporting educational innovation —supporting e-learning —evaluating quality of teaching and assessment • Devising and implementing higher-education policy: —curriculum development —quality assurance	• Newly appointed faculty • Faculty • Teaching assistants • Program directors and committees	• Personal advice and mentoring • Workshops • Programs for specific targeted audiences • Teaching support
Canada	• Mostly centralized units; some partnerships with more locally situated academic units (service and research) • Discipline-specific educational development units in medicine and/or engineering	• Building learning and teaching capacity: —initial and continuing training —consulting —supporting educational innovation —supporting e-learning —evaluating quality of teaching and assessment • Devising and implementing higher-education policy: —curriculum development —quality assurance	• Early-career faculty • Faculty • Graduate students • Program committees and directors • Department chairs	• Personal advice and mentoring • Workshops • Programs for specific targeted audiences • Teaching support

(continued)

TABLE 6.2 (Continued)

	Organizational Structure	Institutional Mandates and Domains of Activity	Targeted Audience	Faculty Development Roles and Strategies
Denmark	• Mostly centralized units; some partnerships with more locally situated academic units (service and research) • Discipline-specific educational development units in engineering and science	• Building learning and teaching capacity: —initial training for mandatory certificate —supporting educational innovation	• New faculty • Subject advisors (experienced faculty)	• Certification in teaching and learning • Workshops • Personal advice and mentoring • Teaching observations
France	• Centralized service units • Discipline-specific educational development units in medicine and/or engineering	• Building learning and teaching capacity: —initial training —supporting e-learning —evaluation of quality of teaching	• New teaching assistants • New faculty	• Workshops
Switzerland	• Centralized units; mainly service-oriented	• Building learning and teaching capacity: —initial and continuing training —consulting —evaluation of quality of teaching and assessment • Devising and implementing higher-education policy: —quality assurance	• Faculty • Teaching assistants • Administrative staff involved in higher-education policy and its implementation	• Workshops • Personal advice and mentoring • Teaching support

faculty development units. Despite the outlined diversities and the varying influences of respective local institutional contexts and traditions, this comparison shows that the faculty development units still share important common characteristics.

Faculty development units are mostly dedicated centralized units within universities, reporting to the vice provost of teaching and learning or his or her equivalent. These units typically share a dual mission: build the learning and teaching capacity of individual teachers and programs within the institution (usually carried out by the teaching or faculty development unit), and devise and implement higher-education policy that arises from national, regional, and/or institutional guidelines (usually undertaken by the educational policy units). In the four European cases included in this book, the ongoing Bologna process is the primary policy influence.

The dual mission results in common domains of activity the units share. Most units offer the complete range of activities toward building learning and teaching: initial and continuing training related to teaching and supervision, consulting, supporting educational innovation and e-learning, and evaluating quality of teaching and assessment of student learning. This pattern is most pronounced in Belgium and Canada, whereas in Switzerland, Denmark, and France, units are more likely to focus on initial and continuing faculty training, and depending on the unit and the faculty developers' expertise, engaging in activities in some other domains (either provide support for educational innovation or evaluate teaching).

Strategies that faculty developers adopt in their interactions are also quite diverse and specific to their domain of activity and target group. The most common ones are one-on-one consulting and mentoring, which sometimes involves classroom observations and videotaping, general workshops on pedagogy targeted for specific groups (for example, graduate/doctoral students and newly appointed faculty), and programs to address specific requests (for example, integrating the use of a particular technology in classes[11]).

Target audiences are broad, since these units direct their activities toward the full range of academic career, from graduate students to experienced faculty. In Belgium, Canada, and Switzerland, faculty development units also provide support to academic administrators, including program and department chairs, program committees, deans, and provosts.

Lessons Learned From Comparison of the Case Studies

The analysis made using the forms of coordination typology reveals common constellations and ways in which they are influencing faculty development policies and practices. Where the state is strongly influential in shaping faculty development or in providing resources and defining all policies, it seems to have an impact as well on the mandate that faculty development units are given. For example, in Denmark, initial pedagogical training is compulsory for new faculty and a condition of being tenured; in France, initial training is compulsory for graduate students who have teaching assistantships.[12] In these instances, activities seem to be more service-oriented and focused on building teaching and learning capacity through initial training and supporting the evaluation of teaching. Faculty development units are less active in supporting innovations, perhaps because innovations are neither defined nor mandated statewide. The state's role and influence, however, can be played down. For instance, Danish universities can fulfill formal requirements for newly appointed faculty through whatever means they choose, with respect to both specific objectives and content, since there is no common national certification qualification. Such autonomy does not exist for French universities, where all initiatives, including creating a faculty development unit, require ministerial approval to obtain special extra funds quadrennially. Therefore, institutionalizing the practice of faculty development depends much more on the will of a specific university and its willingness to dedicate resources than on actions taken at the ministerial or national level.

In contrast, where the state form of coordination has been traditionally less influential (as is the case in Belgium, Switzerland, and Canada), hierarchical organizations have typically had more autonomy, and their faculty development units have had a freer hand to offer a wider range of offerings and activities. Units in these systems also share a common view that service-oriented practices are not enough, and that they need to be research- or evidence-based. One could argue that the influential market form of coordination, which encourages universities to seek ways of attracting faculty and students and ensuring high-quality education, mitigates the investment in faculty development in this more comprehensive format. The market factor is more likely to become even more influential in European countries as the Bologna process continues to unfold and more common policies such as quality assurance become accepted. This is already evident in Belgium and Switzerland, where the state (considered at the level of language and cultural communities or cantons), through new laws and regulations within the Bologna process, is pushing universities to coordinate efforts via associations or networks. This, in turn, is concurrently reducing the autonomy of universities.

In four of the five countries (all except France), the presence of communities of faculty developers is also a feature that stands out. One way to interpret this phenomenon is that where faculty development practices have had a long history, educational developers have felt the need to exchange ideas with colleagues and build a community of practice that can help them withstand potentially diverging constraints and influences from local, institutional, regional, national, or international levels.

Despite the contextual differences of the cases, there is much more similarity in faculty development practices than we would have surmised from simply reading the individual country case studies and investigating their specific higher-education systems. What are some possible explanations?

The first is that institutional and cultural contexts apparently have very little influence on faculty development practices. The second is that existing faculty development practices are based on a common core of knowledge and research, and it is through this scholarship that communities of educational developers share knowledge. The third is that continuous exchanges and professional meetings act as robust conduits for the transfer of models and best practices among faculty developers. We discuss these possibilities below.

Our initial analysis does not completely support the first explanation. From what we have learned from our case studies and analysis of the countries' higher-education systems, institutional, regional, and national cultures and traditions seem to shape policies and practices. These policies define ways of doing and practicing, even when international mainstream policies place strong and sometimes discordant tensions on local cultures and traditions. The influence may emanate from different and multiple levels: disciplinary, institutional, regional (for example, provinces, communities, or cantons), national, or international. Local faculty development units accommodate the influences in their unique way, depending on the power of each level and the unit's so-called breathing space. The result could be similar practices across the country, as is the case in France. However, practices may also vary considerably among regional levels, as is the case in Canada, Belgium, and Switzerland. Even within regional levels (depending on other layers), there may be vast differences in practices. Examples are the educational networks in Belgium and the language and cultural differences in Quebec, compared to other provinces in Canada. The analysis based on Boyer and Hollingsworth's typology has provided considerable information in this regard, and has helped in gaining an understanding of the influential modes of coordination and how they constitute a unique combination. The example of France is especially illustrative: France has long been a centralized state, with all rules and regulations for the governance of higher education, even at the local level, defined by the Minister of Education and issued from Paris. It seems that this state form of coordination, combined with a loose market, explains the relatively low level of faculty development in the country.[13] But this elaboration is not quite enough to understand the actual and relatively underdeveloped landscape of faculty development in France. As described by Paul and Adangnikou (chapter 5), the local and disciplinary culture of the academics and the level of general support for institutional and individual initiatives have played important roles.

The second hypothetical explanation for commonalities among faculty development practices is difficult to take for granted. As elaborated in the chapters on the different case studies and on the conceptual framework, faculty development as a field of practice has not yet established its own stable core theoretical foundation, a necessary condition for unique/similar sets of practices. Moreover, faculty development may not yet even be considered as a profession with all of the formal attributes as defined by Bourdoncle (1991).

The third hypothesis has to do with the transfer of models and practices. One reason why faculty development practices seem lacking in diversity may be because educational developers exchange ideas and ways of practice in professional meetings. Thus, the network form of coordination at a transnational level is a powerful venue for exchanging ideas and may explain some of the commonalities encountered in our case studies. However, the exchange of educational developers' practices and the adjustments they make to what they learn from each other do not provide a satisfactory explanation for this hypothesis. What we have experienced from analyzing both the case studies and the Mobility Project (Frenay et al., 2005) is that differences often are not apparent at first glance. A workshop designed or led by a faculty developer in one country at first may appear not to be much different from a similar workshop in another country. But on closer examination, nuances and finer subtleties become more salient and differences are manifest, especially in the meaning of terms, strategies, and pedagogical methods used to reach a specific target audience (Taylor & Rege Colet, chapter 7).

Our conclusion is that these three sets of explanations, while illuminating, are not enough to explain similarities and differences among observed practices, and to obtain a more complete picture, we need to look between the lines. As Figure 6.3 highlights, building teaching capacity in universities through faculty development practices is totally embedded in contexts and rooted in solid foundations. The unique nature of a faculty development unit comes from the interactions among contexts and foundations and how faculty developers put them into practice to support a central institutional mission. The repercussion is that this also influences its own contexts and the building of common theories and principles for the field of educational development. Therefore, even though each faculty development unit is unique, it shares similar features with other faculty development units and the larger community of faculty developers.

FIGURE 6.3
Building Teaching Capacity in Universities

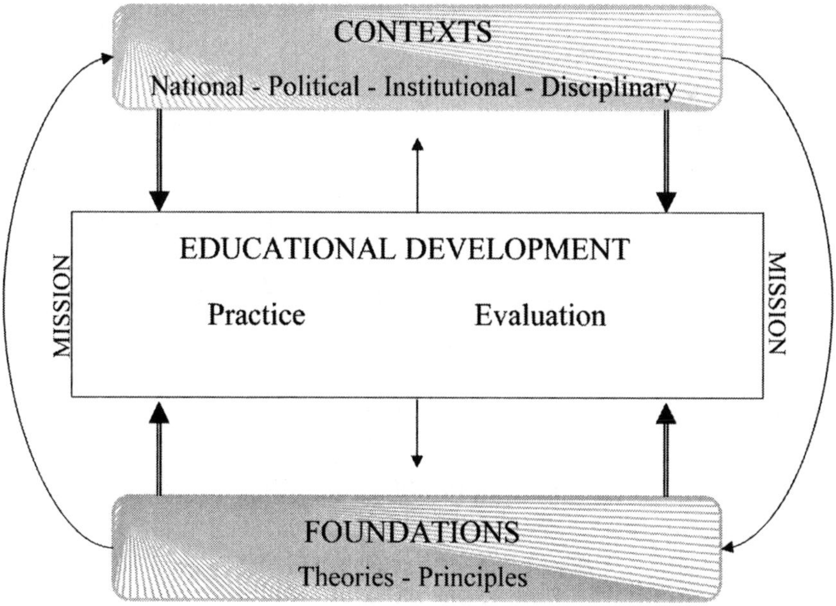

Challenges Facing Educational Development

Faculty and educational development (see Taylor & Rege Colet, chapter 7, for a discussion) is becoming a more visible and valued activity in higher-education institutions due partly to important changes in the European and broader international contexts. Taking into account the broader international context, as well as specific national and regional contexts, through our analysis we have tried to address a fundamental question that is crucial for educational developers: How do we improve and establish the field of research and practice in faculty development so that it becomes essential to answering urgent needs arising from ongoing changes? Moreover, how do we render the practice of faculty development more credible and better informed by research?

Challenges facing educational development as a field of research and practice may then be seen at different levels. First, this field needs to be rooted in strong theoretical and research foundations. At a minimum, this leads to the following challenges:

- need to reconceptualize faculty development to create a core of knowledge and at the same time address discipline-based educational development so it becomes relevant and understandable by various target audiences, and
- need to make faculty development become a topic of inquiry to ensure that good research follows—research that is both theoretical and empirical, and that is disseminated widely. As a field of practice, this research should find its place somewhere between traditional and action-based educational research.

Second, as a field of practice and research, faculty development needs strong scholarly communities. This entails another set of challenges:

- building a so-called new profession by developing scholarly communities to support the work of educational developers, and building communities of practice and scholarship with colleagues so the status and expertise of faculty developers at stake may be recognized, and
- providing initial and continuing development for faculty developers, which starts with recruiting scholars who are willing to become involved in the field to enhance its scholarship and who understand

the pathways into educational development (Chism, 2007; McDonald & Stockley, 2008). Initial and continuing training and development of educational developers needs to be discussed and organized, and the ways and means to fulfill this aspiration are various and need to be considered carefully. For instance, what is to be gained (or lost) from a formal accreditation process (Groccia, Boyd, & St.Clair, 2007)? What are the advantages of collegial forms of training and exchanges (for example, the Mobility Project, FACDEV, which inspired this book; Frenay et al., 2005)?

Third, as a field of practice, faculty development needs to be able to ascertain its relevance and efficacy, which raises important challenges around evaluation of faculty development activities:

- evaluating the impact of educational development on teaching and on learning: This requires developing ecologically valid, reliable, and efficient methods and expertise, and taking into account inputs, processes, outputs, and outcomes associated with teaching as well as student learning;
- addressing the need to analyze effects, not only in answering individual needs (being responsive), but also in being proactive in initiating programs and responding to institutional demands, such as the need to fulfill accreditation and quality assurance requirements; and
- ensuring that, in assessing the quality of universities, in addition to governance and management, student outputs are taken into account—in particular, the quality of learning using qualitative indicators to complement common quantitative measures (for example, time to graduation and ratio of students to faculty). Supporting the development of innovative ways of training (for example, problem-based learning [PBL] in Denmark and teaching soft skills) and evaluating the added value to learning are also ways to promote quality learning.

Fourth, as a field of practice, faculty development needs to be sustainable. This requires that investments in faculty development structures preferably be made long term, but at least mid term, to enable attending to long-term needs and effecting changes in how target audiences conceptualize and practice teaching. Some challenges in this dimension may be:

- generating far-reaching policies that will enable faculty development units to be responsive to all and, in particular, to early-career and newly appointed teaching staff; moreover, to include pedagogical development as an integral component of doctoral education regardless of discipline;
- engaging in a distributed model of faculty development by empowering faculty peers to take on and initiate development responsibilities with their colleagues; and
- allocating resources and ensuring the continued presence of a critical mass in faculty/educational development units, which may help to prevent units from becoming dependent on individuals rather than on the enterprise itself.

Notes

1. Canadian universities have had a tradition of faculty development for several decades.

2. The European Credit Transfer and Accumulation System (ECTS) is a student-centerd system based on the *student workload* required to achieve the objectives of a program, objectives preferably specified in terms of *learning outcomes* and competencies to be acquired. ECTS is based on the principle that 60 credits measure the workload of a full-time student during one academic year. The student workload of a full-time study program in Europe in most cases amounts to 1,500 to 1,800 hours per year, and in these cases, one credit represents 25 to 30 working hours. See http://ec.europa.eu/education/programmes/socrates/ects/index_en.html for ECTS key features.

3. These were adopted two years later in Bergen (ENQA, 2005).

4. Definitions of the elements of Dupriez and Maroy's (2003) model (shown here) are conceptualized after Hollingsworth and Boyer (1997).

- A *market* is defined as a "decentralized localized exchange in which each transactor remains autonomous and defends his or her own interests" (Dupriez & Maroy, 2003, p. 380). In this typology, "markets fall into the upper left quadrant of the diagram, combining a self-interested actor and a relatively horizontal distribution of power" (p. 380).
- A *hierarchy* is a "formal type of organization in which a large part of the decision-making power is centralized at the top" (Dupriez & Maroy, 2003, p. 380). This falls into the upper right quadrant.
- The *state* is a more complex institutional arrangement that differs from other types to the extent that it "sanctions and regulates the various non-state coordinating mechanisms, [and] is the ultimate enforcer of rules of the various mechanisms" (Hollingsworth & Boyer, 1997, p. 13). The state acts as a regulator of last resort and can also

function as a collective actor. This form of coordination is located in the lower right quadrant.

- A *network* is a form of coordination "in which the actors are loosely connected to each other" on a mid- to long-term basis "in a manner that promotes their capacities to work together and cooperate" (Dupriez & Maroy, 2003, p. 381). Repeated exchanges among the same actors forge and reinforce relationships.
- An *association* is similar to a network, but "tends to bring together actors who are engaged in similar activities"; a network tends "to bring together actors who are engaged in complementary activities." These are located in the upper quadrants (the "Interests" side), but "in the centre as regards the distribution of formal power" (Dupriez & Maroy, 2003, p. 381).
- In a *community*, "the actor maintains reciprocal relationships based on trust and interests common to the group" (Dupriez & Maroy, 2003, p. 381). This institutional arrangement occupies the lower left quadrant.

5. In Canada, education falls within provincial jurisdiction.

6. In August, the Government of Quebec introduced Bill 38, a makeover of Bill 107. Like its predecessor, Bill 38 seeks to place government representatives on Quebec university boards of governors and to enlarge their powers so that they will participate in the day-to-day running of Quebec universities and will define explicit performance criteria as well as oversee their implementation.

7. Information about the Canada Research Chairs Program can be obtained at http://www.chairs.gc.ca.

8. An example is recent events surrounding inappropriate and unauthorized overspending at one Quebec university, which has had repercussions on other institutions that have been prudent with their expenditures and scrupulous in their accountability. See the report of *Le groupe de travail sur la gouvernance des universités du Québec* at http://www.igopp.org.

9. These are called *Instituts universitaires technologiques* (IUTs).

10. There is considerable public debate on high dropout rates (Hetzel, 2006).

11. For instance, McGill Teaching and Learning Services is working with its faculty of engineering to enhance interactive teaching using clicker technology.

12. This initial training is offered by *Centres d'initiation à l'enseignement supérieur* (centers for preparation for higher education), organized by the Minister of Education in the 1990s.

13. The recent law on universities will probably have consequences in the coming years since it seeks to give universities more autonomy along with more accountability (*LOI n° 2007-1199 du 10 août 2007 relative aux libertés et responsabilités des universités*).

References

Bologna Declaration. (1999). Retrieved from http://www.bologna-bergen2005.no/ Docs/00-Main_doc/990719BOLOGNA_DECLARATION.PDF.

Bourdoncle, R. (1991). La professionnalisation des enseignants: Analyses sociolo-giques anglaises et americaines [The professionalization of teachers: Sociological analyses of British and American systems]. *Revue Française de Pédagogie, 94,* 73–91.

Bourgeois, E. (2002). *Higher education and research for the ERA: Current trends and challenges for the future.* Luxembourg: Office for Official Publications of the European Communities.

Chism, N. (2007, October). *A professional priority: Preparing future developers.* Paper presented at the 32nd annual meeting of the POD Network, "Purpose, Periphery and Priorities," Pittsburgh, PA.

Clement, M., McAlpine, L., & Waeytens, K. (2004). Fascinating Bologna: Impact on the nature and approach of academic development. *The International Journal for Academic Development, 9*(2), 127–131.

Dupriez, V., & Maroy, C. (2003). Regulation in school systems: A theoretical analy-sis of the structural framework of the school systems in French-speaking Belgium. *Journal of Education Policy, 18*(4), 375–392.

European Association for Quality Assurance in Higher Education (ENQA). (2005). *Standards and guidelines for quality assurance in the European higher education area.* Helsinki: European Association for Quality Assurance in Higher Education.

Eurydice. (2000). *Two decades of reform in higher education in Europe: 1980 onwards.* Brussels, Belgium: Eurydice European Unit.

Eurydice. (2007). *Focus on the structure of higher education in Europe: National trends in the Bologna Process—2006/07.* Brussels, Belgium: Eurydice European Unit.

Frenay, M., Saroyan, A., Clement, M., Kolmos, A., Paul, J.-J., Bédard, D., Taylor, L., & Rege Colet, N. (2005). *FACDEV Program: Promoting faculty development to enhance the quality of learning in higher education.* Bruxelles, Belgium: Euro-pean Union, DG Education and Culture.

Gaff, J. G., & Simpson, R. D. (1994). Faculty development in the United States. *Innovative Higher Education, 18*(3), 167–176.

Global University Network on Innovation (GUNI). (2006). *Higher education in the world 2006: The financing of universities.* Hampshire, UK: Palgrave Macmillan.

Global University Network on Innovation (GUNI). (2007). *Higher education in the world 2007: Accreditation for quality assurance.* Hampshire, UK: Palgrave Macmillan.

Groccia, J., Boyd, D., & St.Clair, K. (2007, October). *Academic developers in higher education: A professional development roadmap.* Paper presented at the 32nd annual meeting of the POD Network, "Purpose, Periphery and Priorities," Pittsburgh, PA.

Hetzel, P. (2006). *De l'université à l'emploi: Rapport final de la Commission du débat national Université-Emploi* [From university to the job: Final report of the Commission of the national debate University-Employment]. Paris: La Documentation française.

Hollingsworth, J. R., & Boyer, R. (1997). *Contemporary capitalism: The embeddedness of institutions.* Cambridge, UK: Cambridge University.

Maroy, C., & Dupriez, V. (2000). La régulation dans les systèmes scolaires. Proposition théorique et analyse du cadre structurel en Belgique francophone [Regulation in school systems: A theoretical analysis of the structural framework of the school systems in French-speaking Belgium]. *Revue Française de Pédagogie, 130,* 73–87.

McDonald, J., & Stockley, D. (2008). Pathways to the profession of educational development: An international perspective. *The International Journal for Academic Development, 13*(3), 213–218.

Salmi, J., & Saroyan, A. (2007). League tables as policy instruments: The political economy of accountability in tertiary education. In Global University Network on Innovation (Ed.), *Higher Education in the World 2007: Accreditation for quality assurance* (pp. 79–89). Hampshire, UK: Palgrave Macmillan.

Saroyan, A., & Amundsen, C. (2004). *Rethinking teaching in higher education.* Sterling, VA: Stylus.

Verhesschen, P., & Verburgh, A. (2004). The introduction of the bachelor-master's structure at the K.U. Leuven: Challenges and opportunities for faculty development. *The International Journal for Academic Development, 9*(2), 133–152.

PART TWO

DEVELOPMENT AND VALIDATION OF A CONCEPTUAL FRAMEWORK

7

MAKING THE SHIFT FROM FACULTY DEVELOPMENT TO EDUCATIONAL DEVELOPMENT

A Conceptual Framework Grounded in Practice

K. Lynn Taylor and Nicole Rege Colet

O ver the past decades, higher-education institutions in many countries have responded to increasing public expectations by seriously addressing the issue of quality in postsecondary teaching. One widespread strategy is to launch special units charged with promoting an institutional environment that supports the development of more effective learning and teaching. Whether in educational policy offices or development units, an emerging group of academic professionals is engaged in a range of activities that come under the rubric of developing learning and teaching capacity in postsecondary institutions (Fletcher & Patrick, 1998; Wright, 1995). This thriving community of practice is accumulating a body of knowledge ranging from the wisdom of practice to published research.

However, like many fields of scholarship situated in practice, much of the knowledge generated through practice is created in local contexts, where new understandings, approaches, and terminology emerge as colleagues collaborate with each other, or with a teaching and learning specialist, to achieve more effective learning experiences. The local genesis of this knowledge is both an advantage and a challenge. Because initiatives to develop learning and teaching capacity are now embraced and supported across disciplines, practical and theoretical knowledge is being generated at an exponential rate. While this is all good news, advancing our work as a field of practice and scholarship depends on commitment of the practice community to meet the challenges of sharing, critically examining, and synthesizing locally developed knowledge of teaching and learning in higher education. It is only through sharing this distributed knowledge and expertise that we can contribute to a collective body of practical and conceptual knowledge. As Palmer (1998) reminds us, these efforts are essential to developing practice:

> The growth of any craft depends on shared practice and honest dialogue among the people who do it. We grow by trial and error to be sure—but our willingness to try, and fail, as individuals, is severely limited when we are not supported by a community that encourages such risks. (p. 144)

Efforts to make sense of the experience and knowledge of collective practice and research are also critical to the evolution of learning and teaching development as a field of scholarship. Rowland (1999) argues that "the development of new practices and more developed theories" (p. 312) depends on a three-way interaction among the "personal context" of practice, the "public context" of theory, and the "shared context" of critical debate in a community of discourse. In this interaction, theory is tested and made meaningful in practice, and is subsequently integrated in personal conceptualizations of practice. Similarly, discussions in a shared context refine practice and theory and create new links to practice. The five case studies included in this book and the comparative chapter illustrate evidence of sound local practice in the field of learning and teaching development.

The purpose of this chapter is to draw on the knowledge generated in each of these national contexts to construct a practice-grounded conceptual framework for building learning and teaching capacity. This framework can be examined through the public context of theory and, in turn, can foster a shared context of the larger practice community to help us better understand and advance our still-emerging field.

Several arguments support the need for a comprehensive conceptual framework of learning and teaching development. First, there is a vital need to better understand which such development involves the most effective approaches to development practice. Such an understanding should offer an inclusive framework for analyzing and conceptualizing practice across diverse institutional contexts (Rowland, 1999). Second, a conceptual framework can support the evolution of learning and teaching development as a field of practice and scholarship by guiding the initial and continuing education of educational developers (Sell & Chism, 1991) and by framing research in the field (Brew, 2002). Third, in response to long-standing calls for evidence of the impact of teaching development programs (Levinson-Rose & Menges, 1981; Steinert, 2000; Weimer & Lenze, 1991), a valid framework can be used to construct the evaluation of programs intended to develop learning and teaching. Because the framework presented here is grounded in our five national contexts, we expect that, while it represents our own experience and expertise, it is not yet comprehensive. We invite colleagues to contribute to the elaboration and testing of this framework as a conceptual tool through which we can better understand, implement, and assess learning and teaching development programs.

The Shift From Faculty Development to Educational Development

If you are reading this book in sequence, you no doubt have noted that this chapter makes a shift away from using the term *faculty development*. This shift was, in fact, the first major result of our efforts to integrate collective knowledge from our personal contexts of practice. Through our work in the shared context of this project, we confronted at an early stage the diversity of ways we define our work as "faculty developers." When we turned to the public context of scholarship in the field, we discovered an abundant literature defining faculty development, but no common definition of the concept. A survey of available print and online sources (Land, 2004; Mac-Donald, 2002; Professional and Organizational Network in Higher Education [POD], 2002b; Sorcinelli, Austin, Eddy, & Beach, 2006; Webb, 1996; Wright, 1995) revealed that there is a lack of consensus on what constitutes faculty development. This observation speaks to the powerful influence of institutional context on definitions: the meaning and scope of faculty development is a negotiated phenomenon and can vary widely across institutional environments.

In part because of the context-specific array of meanings attached to the term, there is a rich lexicon associated with faculty development. To understand our eventual choice of terminology, it is useful to examine the scope and articulation of related terms, including instructional development, curriculum development, professional development, organizational development, and academic development. All of these processes relate to enhancing specific dimensions of the academic career experience.

Instructional development is mainly concerned with enhancing course design to support student learning. Improvements concentrate on framing appropriate learning objectives and outcomes; redesigning teaching methods and strategies; reconsidering student assessment and course evaluation; and, in the end, achieving constructive alignment to foster students' learning. The focus is practical with a strong emphasis on more technical aspects of developing teaching and pedagogical planning skills (Mathis, 1979; Wilcox, 1997). Historically, this approach characterized early teacher training programs in many higher-education institutions.

Curriculum development focuses on the development of programs of study (Cook, 2000). In higher education, this approach is about implementing national or local reforms; responding to new demands and needs in higher education; identifying new scientific domains; defining the goals of instruction; selecting and designing the courses or learning modules that fit the curriculum and enable achievement of the learning objectives; making the most of available resources; and monitoring implementation and outcomes (Diamond, 1998; Stark & Lattuca, 1997). For instance, in Europe, the Bologna process (Bologna Declaration, 1999) has shed new light on curriculum development, orienting it toward specific learning outcomes, and this is now a high priority on most higher-education policy agendas. Reshaping higher education on both sides of the Atlantic has given additional weight to curriculum development and has raised the profile of the roles of educational development/policy offices.

Organizational development is about maximizing an institution's resources to meet organizational objectives and to achieve broad institutional missions by supporting policymakers and decision makers in their strategic planning and implementation regarding learning and teaching (Diamond, 2005; Lieberman, 2005; POD, 2002b). Organizational development programs focus on institutional policies and structures for the purpose of generating institutional environments—physical, intellectual, and administrative—that support the development of learning and teaching capacity. Activities include managing institutional change; dealing with governance, including faculty colleagues, when making important decisions regarding organization of learning and teaching; acknowledging and rewarding excellence in teaching; and generally creating work environments that foster effective learning and teaching.

Professional development, when used in reference to the career development of faculty members, focuses on each faculty member as a person and is concerned with his or her development as a scholar (Centra, 1989). In Australasian and British contexts, the term *academic development* is used more commonly to describe the holistic development of academic careers, and implies an integration of personal, professional, and organizational development across the full spectrum of academic work (Brew & Boud, 1996; Candy, 1996). In North America, it is more common to apply the term *faculty development* to this holistic approach (POD, 2002b). In addition to learning and teaching, professional, academic, and (increasingly) faculty development programs deal with career planning and support for scholarly skills such as obtaining research grants, publishing, and supervising scientific activities. Programs might also include communication and managerial skills and time management. While professional development focuses on the development of the person, the scope of academic and faculty development also includes organizational development. Not all higher-education institutions have invested in these more holistic approaches.

The perspective adopted in the current conceptual framework focuses on the development of learning and teaching capacity as an *educational development* process—"all the work that is done systematically to help faculty members to do their best to foster student learning" (Knight & Wilcox, 1998, p. 98). Although educational development is a most widely used term only in Canada (Wilcox, 1997), it was the most suitable term to capture the essence of the roles the five case studies describe.

What does it mean to build learning and teaching capacity through educational development? At the level of individual teachers, Kreber (2002) provides a useful framework for understanding three dimensions of teaching development: excellence in teaching, expertise in teaching, and scholarship of teaching. *Excellence in teaching* is achieved through successful and effective teaching performance that leads to meaningful and lasting learning. Given the fact that most academics do not have extensive preservice opportunities to learn to become good teachers, many educational development activities offer opportunities, including course and curriculum design, to learn, practice, and improve teaching skills (Saroyan & Amundsen, 2004).

Teaching expertise implies knowledge about learning and teaching drawn from both evidence-based sources and experiential learning. Educational development activities promote dissemination of research-based knowledge about learning and teaching, reflection on teaching experience, and self-regulation processes that contribute to the construction of expert knowledge on learning and teaching.

Finally, the *scholarship of teaching* entails sharing knowledge about learning and teaching in forms that can be peer-reviewed on the same terms as any inquiry-based knowledge. Educational development can also support colleagues from across disciplines in systematic inquiry into practice and help disseminate what is learned to the broader academic community.

At the levels of academic units and institutions in these five case studies, building learning and teaching capacity though educational development also means helping institutions to provide the conditions for teachers to recognize the learning needs of students, to acquire a sound knowledge about learning and teaching, to share knowledge in an academic community, and to be recognized and rewarded for their work. Consequently, educational development can span the whole range of approaches described: instructional, curriculum, organizational, and professional/academic/faculty development. Educational development is characterized not by a particular activity such as curriculum development, but by the focus of the range of development activities that are applied and that work in synergy to strengthen learning and teaching capacity. This conceptualization of educational development is elaborated in the description of the conceptual framework that follows.

The Framework

The conceptual framework we propose in this chapter results from an international comparison of a wide range of educational development activities carried out in five countries, and is informed by the existing literature on learning and teaching development and the shared expertise of participants in a Canada–EU mobility project (see Frenay & Saroyan, chapter 6 for more information).

- The framework, grounded in the contextual influences shaping higher-education policy and practice, explains how institutional responses to these influences define the primary missions and scope of the educational development role.

- From this articulation of missions evolve guiding principles, values, scope of practice, and ethics that define educational development as a field of practice and scholarship.
- Within this broad contextual and intellectual framework, educational development practice is a function of specific organizational structures comprising strategies and based on expertise of local educational developers.
- The comprehensive conceptualization of the educational development role and the expertise needed for it lead to valid approaches for evaluating the impact of educational development.

By taking this situated approach regarding understanding, researching, developing, and assessing educational development, it is possible to conceptualize major dimensions of development that cross cultures, institutions, and disciplines. We elaborate the primary components of the framework below.

Educational Development Context and Mission

Across the five case studies, national initiatives to improve the quality and cost-effectiveness of postsecondary education are influencing educational development practice. Political priorities to enhance the accountability of postsecondary systems (for example, recent talk of an international accreditation space), curriculum reform (for example, the Bologna Declaration), more diverse student populations, student access and mobility, and integration of technology have raised the profile and the involvement of educational developers in academic communities (Austin, 2002; Canadian Council on Learning, 2006; Fletcher & Patrick, 1998).

A second dimension of context is that the specific form of involvement in educational development varies across disciplines. Every discipline is shaped by a discourse community characterized by shared goals and values; processes of critical inquiry, reflection, and analysis; a shared "discursive practice" (Swales, 1990) and language (which may or may not be transparent to other communities of discourse); and collective work toward building knowledge in a domain, including knowledge about learning and teaching in that discipline (Brew, 1999; Huber, 2004; Rice, 1996; Shulman, 2002;

Swales, 1990).Within each disciplinary community, the language and pro-cesses of engaging in the common goal of improving learning and teaching will differ (Becher & Trowler, 2001; Eimers, 1999; Stark & Lattuca, 1997).

These national and disciplinary contexts come together in particular institutional contexts, each with its own values, history, and priorities. It is at the institutional level that the contextual vectors such as curriculum design support and institutional policies with respect to learning and teaching inter-sect to produce a local work environment that strongly influences educa-tional development practice (Kember, 1997; Light, Drane, & Calkins, 2005). Promoting the learning and teaching agenda in universities necessarily takes place within varied contexts. Effective educational development practice depends on a deep appreciation of how the local context of our work is con-structed as well as the ability to communicate successfully in that context (Dall'Alba & Sandberg, 2006; Steinert, 2000; Taylor, 2005).

Across the five case studies, there was a shared dual mission for educa-tional development: to enhance learning and teaching capacity, and to advo-cate for the quality of the student learning experience. With respect to enhancing the learning experience at universities, the educational develop-ment mission emphasizes concrete actions and offers a clear view of the focal point of the educational development mission: building learning and teach-ing capacity among individual teachers, programs, and institutions. How-ever, the purpose of educational development programs in these five cases is also to advocate for the quality of learning and teaching through policymak-ing, resource allocation, and strategic reward structures. Advocacy is particu-larly important in research-intensive institutions where there may be little incentive to engage in the educational component of the professorial man-date. This dual mission demands a complex skill set that integrates many of the approaches to educational development identified by Land (2004): competency in the domain of educational development, manager, diplomat/politician/strategist, researcher, and opportunist.

Guiding Principles, Values, and Ethics of Educational Development Practice

Most educational developers are guided in their practice by the principles underpinning their work and by the objectives of their programs. The Pro-fessional and Organizational Network in Higher Education (POD, 2002b) in the United States and the Staff and Educational Development Association

(Staff and Educational Development Network [SEDA], 2005) in Great Britain are among the professional associations that articulate the values that characterize the commitment toward learning and teacher training for higher education and educational development. The values expressed in their foundational work are reflected in common principles observed across the five practice contexts in this project: working in the local context, using and generating evidence-based knowledge, maintaining a focus on learning, and respecting collegiality. These findings are consistent with those expressed in the broader literature on the principles that underlie the practice and scholarship of educational development (Brew & Boud, 1996; Candy, 1996; Chism, Lees, & Evenbeck, 1998; Gandolfo, 1997; Hart, 1997; Knight & Wilcox, 1998; Sorcinelli et al., 2006; Steinert, 2000).

Contextualized Nature of Development

One of the dominant themes shared by the five case studies and evidenced in the educational development literature is the importance of appreciating and working in the local context. This principle implies a comprehensive knowledge of the community in which one works (Taylor, 2005), a commitment to the priorities and needs of individuals and groups in that community (Candy, 1996; Steinert, 2000), and the ability to balance the conflicting priorities that inevitably emerge (Knight & Wilcox, 1998). Even within an institution, knowing one's context requires more than passive observation; it requires active participation in the community and sharing issues, challenges, and resources with multiple audiences (Palmer, 1998).

Evidence-Based Practice

Effective educational development programs draw on and contribute to evidence-based knowledge. Given the scope of practice, the base of potential evidence ranges from learning and teaching theory to academic culture, leadership, and change theory (Gandolfo, 1997; Schönwetter & Taylor, 2003; Sorcinelli et al., 2006; Steinert, 2000). Evidence-based knowledge also informs the processes that characterize educational development practice: interpreting concepts and research findings in different disciplines (Wareing, 2004), collaborative learning and problem solving (Candy, 1996; Stevenson, Duran, Barrett, & Colarulli, 2005; Taylor, 2005), and integrating rather than asserting expertise (Taylor, 2005). In the five case studies and in the broader research literature, systematic use of sound research and best practices raises the credibility and impact of educational development practice.

Focus on Learning

The focus on learning valued in the five case studies is also reflected in the educational development literature. Most contemporary programs in higher education explicitly foster a change of perspective from the traditional teacher-centered knowledge dissemination to a learning-centered approach (Chism et al., 1998; Sorcinelli et al., 2006). This implies a better understanding of learning: how students learn, the conditions that facilitate learning, and how to enhance students' active engagement in learning. This learning perspective also applies to the relationships between good teaching and effective learning. Increasingly, faculty are encouraged to engage in practice-driven inquiry into a range of teaching issues to learn how to better facilitate the student learning experience (Hutchings & Shulman, 1999). This learning perspective on both the objectives and the processes of educational development brings a much-needed unifying framework to the diverse activities educational developers engage in.

Collegiality

Across the five case studies and in the broader experience, educational development is optimized when collegiality characterizes individual initiatives and the general relationships among educational developers and teachers, professors, students, administrative and technical personnel, and academic administrators (Gandolfo, 1997). Within collegial initiatives, participants frequently engage in collaborative learning with one another and with developers (Scott & Weeks, 1996; Taylor, 2005; Wildman, Hable, Preston, & Magliaro, 2000). This reciprocal approach requires sound teamwork and an infrastructure within which all partners can contribute their expertise to the problem-solving/improvement process. Within this process, participants may have different beliefs, conceptions, and knowledge about learning and teaching. It is essential to encourage open discussions among partners and to enable them to challenge evidence-based and experiential knowledge in scholarly and respectful ways.

Educational development is not about making sure that everyone arrives at the same level of sophistication in the most efficient way (Dall'Alba & Sandberg, 2006). Within the broad principles of learning and teaching, there are many ways to be an effective teacher, and individual teachers develop at individual paces and according to personal objectives. Across the case studies, it was important for educational developers to maintain collegiality when counseling individual faculty members or teams, providing constructive feedback, or suggesting new paths or directions for their work. Collegiality is also essential while devising and implementing institutional strategies or advising academic administrators. Sharing learning and teaching expertise and experiences across disciplines and functions in higher education will not only help build knowledge and learning and teaching capacity, but it will also foster the interdisciplinary community building that characterizes effective institutions (Senge, 1999).

Ethics

Maintaining collegiality across many different local and institutional contexts while upholding a commitment to evidence-based learning and teaching practice is not without its challenges (Knight & Wilcox, 1998). Like other professionals, educational developers in these five case studies appeal to the ethics and values that guide the profession when inevitable tensions emerge between individual and institutional goals and between the teaching mission and the multiple responsibilities of academic life and when implementing evidence-based practices across the cultures of different disciplines. Many of these ethical values are shared with faculty colleagues, as Gandolfo's (1997) application of *Ethical Principles in University Teaching* to development practice well illustrates. In the United States, the Professional and Organizational Network in Higher Education published *Ethical Guidelines for Educational Developers* (POD, 2002a), under which educational developers maintain their personal and professional integrity by:

- articulating clear roles and obligations to all partners;
- being critically aware of the knowledge and skills required for competent practice, developing and elaborating this knowledge base, and exercising this knowledge in the interests of one's professional mission and the needs of clients;
- protecting clients' rights to diverse values and different approaches to learning and teaching;
- maintaining confidentiality with respect to client identity and information within legal regulations; and
- contributing to the development of the practice and scholarship of educational development by sharing knowledge and advocating for development.

While these principles have their own inherent challenges (Gandolfo, 1997), the evolution of the educational development role in directions that include institutional as well as individual development further complicates ethical practice (Knight & Wilcox, 1998). As institutions experience greater demands for accountability, the expertise of educational developers is increasingly needed to facilitate change to achieve educational goals at the institutional level (for example, improving students' engagement in learning), at the national level (for example, improving teaching quality), or at the international level (for example, aligning curricula to meet requirements of the Bologna process). Although all of these initiatives have value, the tensions between individuals' academic freedom and institutional priorities make the negotiated path to ethical practice that much more complex (Knight & Wilcox, 1998).

Educational Development Units

Institutional Mandates

Within the conceptual parameters of educational development and the principles and ethics of practice, the concrete roles and structures of educational development units can take different organizational forms depending on the local context. As we mentioned previously, most universities now have a specialized unit dedicated to university learning and teaching. Across the five case studies, these units fall under two general categories: educational policy offices and educational development units. Educational policy offices primarily devise and implement higher-education policy that arises from national, regional, and/or institutional guidelines. For instance, in Europe, educational policy offices are particularly involved in implementing the principles of the Bologna process. In contrast, educational development units are more concerned about building the learning and teaching capacity of individual teachers and programs within the institution. Throughout higher-education institutions, educational development units come under a wide range of designations, the most common being centers for university learning and teaching, learning and teaching support services, learning and teaching development units, higher-education development units, and staff and educational development centers. Whatever the variant, the focus on *teaching* and *learning* is explicit.

As the analysis of the five case studies indicates (Frenay & Saroyan, chapter 6), the explicit mandate of educational development can include planning and coordinating teacher training activities; disseminating evidence-based information to inform effective learning and teaching; organizing evaluation procedures on quality of teaching and evaluation; and consulting with individual academics and institutional authorities on learning and teaching issues. Some units also support the appropriate use of technology to enhance learning and teaching. Several institutions have put together funds to support and reward pedagogical initiatives and rely on their educational development units for designing programs, selecting projects for funding, and monitoring progress. Most recently, educational development units have become involved in fostering the scholarship of teaching and learning by supporting colleagues in planning systematic inquiry into teaching issues and disseminating the results (Huber & Hutchings, 2005). Across the five case studies, five domains of activity summed up the educational mandate of many educational development units: training, evaluating, consulting, supporting e-learning and other forms of innovation, and facilitating the scholarship of teaching and learning. The emphasis on each of these dimensions varies from one center to another, depending on explicit mandates and resources made available.

Organizational Structure

Across the five cases studies, educational development centers were usually situated as centralized units directly attached to a senior administrative position in the rector's/president's office with responsibility for learning and teaching. This centralized organizational structure sets the units apart from traditional academic reporting lines and situates them in a reporting pattern similar to other university services, such as computer services, financial services, and personnel services. However, because most centers endeavor to disseminate and build research-based knowledge and expertise to enhance learning and teaching, educational development is situated in the domain of academic work, even when there is no explicit mandate concerning research on higher education. As a result, many centralized educational development centers seek out partnerships with more locally situated academic units. To meet specific needs, a center may allocate an educational developer tasked with providing dedicated development resources to an academic unit while maintaining regular contact with the educational development center.

Alternatively, regular faculty members may be appointed as learning and teaching advisors or to committees that then work closely with the centers. Regardless of the specific strategy, the general idea is to build strategic bridges between the centralized and local levels of educational development. These collaborations lead to joint research projects and joint ventures in teacher training activities and mentorship and involve academics in the work of centers.

Few institutions have the resources to set up educational development centers for each faculty or academic school, although academics and educational developers may claim that the need for discipline-specific educational development is strong. One exception to this general observation is faculties of medicine, which have developed their own units for medical education. Across the five case studies, medical educational development has become a field of its own with a distinct community and network that tend to develop parallel development perspectives, although both share many objectives and ambitions.

Target Audiences

Across the five case studies, educational development services are generally available to every member of the academic community, but, in fact, junior teaching staff represent the largest target audience. Less-experienced colleagues with little prior training in the field and who are suddenly faced with teaching responsibilities are motivated to participate in programs and obtain assistance in facing their new challenges. This explains why an increasing number of educational development programs are specially designed for early-career academics to introduce them to a professional development pathway that will combine research and teaching rather than maintain the schism between the two activities (Austin, 2002; Gaff, 2002).

A second emerging target group is the increasing proportion of adjunct or associated faculty colleagues who may not be full-time educators, but nonetheless have a number of unique development needs, including socialization to the institution, knowledge about the programs and cultures in which they teach, and connecting with the academic community in which they work, as well as their long-term career development (Gappa & Leslie, 1993; Lyons, 2004).

Graduate students represent a third target group. Increasingly, educational development activities are being integrated into graduate programs. A range of educational development initiatives prepare graduate students for immediate teaching roles as lecturers, tutorial leaders, lab assistants, and graders/markers as well as for their future roles as researchers who will also act as educators in a wide range of settings that comprise the knowledge-based society, including academic environments (Marincovich, Prostko, & Stout, 1998; Schönwetter & Taylor, 2003). These initiatives both span and integrate diverse learning experiences that include individual workshops; seminars; and consultations, graduate courses, and full certificates and diplomas.

Experienced faculty represent a fourth target group. More experienced colleagues, while not the primary educational development audience, are an important clientele. These colleagues have different learning needs. Many senior colleagues remain interested in teaching but have fewer opportunities to engage in discussion or to undertake initiatives in their classrooms (LaCelle-Peterson & Finkelstein, 1993; Romano, Hoesing, O'Donovan, & Weinsheimer, 2004). Karpiak (1997) pinpointed the mid-career isolation of experienced colleagues and the importance of remaining part of an academic community and fulfilling one's sense of doing work that "matters." Blaisdell and Cox (2004) make a case for reengaging these senior colleagues in faculty learning communities to draw on their considerable experience and knowledge and to involve them in the educational development process. Such colleagues are also well positioned to participate productively in peer consultations, mentoring, faculty discussion groups, and curriculum redesign.

Roles and Strategies

Educational development centers use a wide range of strategies to fulfill their mandates. Teacher development may range from individual workshops to comprehensive programs to postgraduate programs in university learning and teaching. Mentoring programs are also available to help novice teachers develop their teaching practice through regular contacts with experienced teachers. The centers also offer consultation on an individual or departmental level. Individual consultations may deal with issues such as course design, teaching skills, innovative teaching, e-learning, and student assessment and may involve classroom observations focused on teaching development.

At the department or program level, consultations with an educational developer can focus on designing and redesigning programs and courses, allocating teaching resources, evaluating student workload, maximizing collaboration, and balancing student assessment methods. Educational developers also provide advice on the formative and summative evaluation of individual courses or programs, and developers occasionally will help organize external reviews or benchmarking exercises.

At the institutional level, developers participate in establishing mission statements, policies, and procedures that recognize and reward teaching in the allocation of faculty work, and they influence how faculty performance is evaluated and rewarded through promotion, tenure, and awards. They can also contribute their expertise to designing physical and online learning environments. While creating administrative and physical infrastructure to support learning and teaching is essential to building individual and institutional capacity, so is establishing a communications infrastructure that effectively carries information about resources, policies and their implementation, and awards to both internal and external audiences. In the five case studies, educational developers played important advocacy roles in ensuring that both substantive and strategic messaging reaches intended audiences.

In all of these roles, the work of educational developers is situated as academic work. Regardless of whether developers hold academic or administrative positions, they need to be seen as engaging in academic work (Taylor, 2005) for credibility and validity. Ideally, their work is characterized as an inquiry process shared with a community of colleagues invested in the common goal of creating more effective student learning experiences.

Expertise of Educational Developers

Despite the complexity of the field, there are few formal training programs to become an educational developer. Like many of the participants in this project, colleagues come to educational development roles from associated fields but without direct preparation. For instance, a recent survey (Centre for University Teaching [CUT], 2006) of 50 educational developers who work in Quebec and French-speaking European universities revealed that a majority held a postgraduate degree in either psychology or educational sciences. However, one-third of these educational developers came to educational development from a totally different field. In a domain where many practitioners learn from experience, the rapid expansion of the practice community means that many educational developers have little experience on which to draw. In a larger North American study, more than half of the almost 500 respondents had less than five years' experience (Sorcinelli et al., 2006). This profile, together with the broad scope of educational development practice, suggests that both preservice and continuing professional development programs focusing on a number of key areas would serve the community well.

Understanding Learning and Teaching

Whatever their backgrounds, educational developers no doubt become experts in a wide range of fields that inform the work of educational development. First of all, educational developers require a deep understanding of learning and teaching. This comprises evidence-based knowledge about the multiple dimensions of teaching practice, approaches for preparing teachers for effective learning and teaching, insights on student learning and motivation, and the conditions that support the learning process (Sorcinelli et al., 2006).

Developers also need to know how faculty develop as teachers (Amundsen, Saroyan, & Gryspeerdt, 1999; Fulton & Licklider, 1998) and, in particular, the nature of faculty learning in professional development situations (Tiberius, Smith, & Waisman, 1998). Evidence-based approaches mean that developers need to be in constant contact with the most recent research data on learning and teaching, draw on major results and conclusions in their everyday practice, and share the information with colleagues in the disciplines who, as researchers, are used to referring to the theoretical and empirical literature to guide their actions.

Understanding Academic Culture

The central position of educational development units enables developers to construct a better grasp of academic culture, since institutional and disciplinary differences are not only identified, but also taken into account when devising learning and teaching projects and activities (Becher & Trowler, 2001; Hativa & Marincovich, 1995; Middendorf & Pace, 2004; Neuman, Parry, & Becher, 2002). University learning and teaching centers are prominent observatories of academic life, and developers accumulate unique information about disciplinary issues and institutional traditions. How do disciplinary cultures affect teaching and teachers' personal epistemology? What is the weight of departmental traditions and habits where teaching is concerned? These observations encourage educational developers to examine the influence of discipline-specific pedagogical knowledge (Huber & Morreale, 2002; Shulman, 1987) for understanding learning and teaching in higher education, and to test models that define this pedagogical knowledge and describe how pedagogical knowledge and expertise grow in different disciplines. Based on the five case studies and on the broader literature, an understanding of academic cultures is essential to the role of an educational developer.

Leadership

Developmental work carried out daily requires relevant knowledge about leadership and how it functions in particular settings (Taylor & Schönwetter, 2002). Educational developers can often identify major change agents and their own leadership roles in promoting and sustaining the development of learning and teaching in their academic communities. They use this information to support institutional strategies and encourage innovators and academic leaders. As Taylor (2005, pp. 43–44) observed:

Developers reflect effective leadership when they:

- Listen, appreciate, and use internal and external contexts, recognize problems and opportunities, consult, generate vision in harmony with community, are aware of established conventions, communicate effectively, and align beliefs and action (Kouzes & Posner, 1995; Ramsden, 1998).
- Seize teaching opportunities, set clear goals, help others achieve goals, enable others to act, encourage efforts, provide feedback, lead by example, and foster professional development (Kouzes & Posner, 1995; Leithwood, 1992; Ramsden, 1998).
- Recogniz[e] opportunities to learn and improve, collaborat[e], form . . . partnerships, shar[e] responsibility, consult . . . , combin[e] ideas, respect . . . autonomy, learn . . . from others, and learn . . . from experience (Ramsden, 1998).
- [Build] shared goals, find . . . common purpose, nurtur[e] mutual trust, support . . . reciprocity, sustain . . . interaction, believ[e] in others, enabl[e] others to act, and help . . . people solve problems together (Kouzes & Posner, 1995; Leithwood, 1992; Senge, 1990).

Across the five case studies, the regular contacts developers maintained with academic and administrative authorities also enabled them to take part in building the vision for learning and teaching in their institutions. Educational developers need to know about guiding and facilitating change, how to give judicious advice without alienating the teaching staff, and how to bring people together over a common goal, to lead work groups, to facilitate the learning of teaching staff, and to manage large-scale projects.

Development of Expertise

Analyzing the expertise of educational developers helps to identify the competencies and skills that comprise professional practice. Based on this analysis, it is possible to build a framework for initial and continuous education in educational development and to set the learning objectives of such programs (SEDA, 2005). Although many universities offer postgraduate courses in university teaching to doctoral students and junior teaching staff, there are few opportunities such as those offered through the project examined in the introduction of this volume to undertake academic preparation for the educational development role. Developing a competency map such as the one that emerged from this project (Figure 7.1) can help define the core curriculum for the broader educational development community.

In the interim, continuing professional development provides the major learning opportunity for new and more experienced educational developers. As in other professions, professional development is something educational developers provide for each other through conferences, workshops, and professional development programs. Under these circumstances, the scholarly and professional infrastructure of regional, national, and international academic societies; listservs, online communities of practice; conferences; and meetings is critical to ongoing growth of educational development as a field of practice and scholarship.

Evaluating the Impact of Educational Development

Underlying educational development programs is the assumption that educational development has a significant impact on building learning and teaching capacity. The most important challenge developers in the five case studies now face is providing evidence that there is a relationship between their activities and improvements and/or changes in both the conception and practice of teaching. What evidence do we have that educational development is truly effective and achieves the goals set by both educational

FIGURE 7.1

An Emerging Educational Development Competency Framework

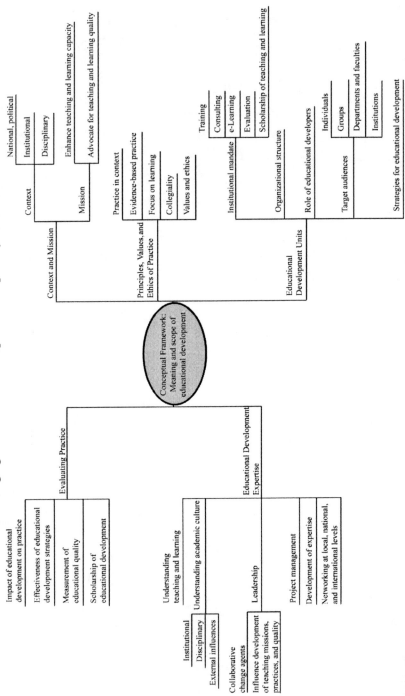

developers and the institution? What evidence do we have that this process is efficient, cost-effective, and justifiable in this age when there are competing demands for resources? Given that educational development is one place removed from most learning experiences, what impact can this work claim to produce (Knight & Wilcox, 1998)?

To grow as a field of practice and scholarship, educational development initiatives must provide a public account of activities and outcomes and a rigorous analysis of field research conducted according to academic standards. The results of this research will demonstrate accountability, promote the roles of educational development, gain recognition for work carried out, and contribute to expert knowledge about building learning and teaching capacity in academic communities. Until now there has been little research in this direction (Chism & Szabo, 1996; Steinert, 2000; Weimer & Lenze, 1991), and educational developers cannot easily rely on empirical evidence to affirm the validity of educational development.

As the field matures, the notion of an expanding base of educational development scholarship becomes a valuable resource. As with scholarship of learning and teaching, such scholarship implies a conceptual framework for evaluating impact, a robust methodology to collect relevant data, and the results of academic work that are reported in peer-reviewed formats according to customary scientific and academic standards (Glassick, Huber, & Maeroff, 1997).

In response to internal quality assurance procedures and external reviews of educational development units and programs, research on educational development in higher education and systematic evaluation of educational development initiatives should be high on the agenda. Networking on an international scale is going to be essential to evaluate effectiveness and to design appropriate research programs. The purpose of evaluating the impact of educational development goes beyond simply filling an evidence gap and building significant information to support the adoption of beneficial practices. It also allows educational development to make a huge leap forward and to become a research-based field of knowledge and practice in the realm of higher education.

Conclusion

The Mobility Project discussed in this volume was undertaken with a strong practice orientation. We believed that by systematically observing, sharing, and analyzing our respective national perspectives on educational development practice, each country's practice would benefit. In the shared experience of the project, we soon realized the synergy of the interaction of Rowland's (1999) private (practice), public (theory), and shared (critical debate) contexts. As we confronted differences in our national contexts, practice missions, and strategies, there were many hours of critical reflection and discussion about the practices, principles, values, and concepts that we had largely taken for granted in the private contexts of practice. From this process evolved new understandings of the scope and meaning of educational development, some of the tensions underlying practice, and some challenges for the future.

With respect to the scope and meaning of educational development, the challenge of articulating and debating the knowledge of our field yielded new insights about the substance and structure of our collective knowledge, represented in its current form in the competency map (Figure 7.1). The components of the conceptual framework and the competency map represent broadly shared insights about our practice, appreciated further in the context of the larger literature in the field and through critical reflection and discussion. The framework and the map are still works in progress, but they have already informed how each of us understands, articulates, implements, and assesses our work. Developing the conceptual framework and competency map not only has produced a comprehensive model for understanding and analyzing our experiences in educational development practice, but it also has articulated the foundation for conceptualizing our professional knowledge.

Furthermore, the process of analyzing our experiences has revealed some of the tensions that characterize our work. The primary sources of tension in all case studies were the gaps and mismatches between espoused institutional values and the day-to-day practices related to learning and teaching. Learning may feature prominently in our mission statements and recruitment brochures, but are normative practices through which faculty work is assigned, recognized, and rewarded in alignment with these value statements? A second set of tensions evolves from perceived gaps between investments in learning and teaching development at the institutional and individual levels. With increasing demands on institutions to offer quality education, demonstrate accountability, and engage in particular curriculum reforms such as the Bologna process, resources available for individual development are limited. These tensions raise important questions about the missions of educational development units, particularly for those units that traditionally have focused on the development of individuals based on personal development needs. A third source of tension is the unprecedented pressure for change. Across the five case studies, shifts in accountability, diversity of the student body, new technology, limited resources for higher education, and how we understand the learning process have all converged to create changing expectations for the education mission and for faculty roles and responsibilities. When this changing learning environment is combined with stretched development resources and misaligned values and rewards, the level of tension in the system proliferates.

In addition to responding to these immediate tensions, what long-term challenges lie ahead? From our perspective, the most significant challenge is to develop methods and expertise to support evaluation of the educational development programs' impact on the learning of faculty members and their students. This priority evolved from a growing need to demonstrate the value of our work in the academy, as other domains of academic work are expected to do. Perhaps even more important is the fact that responding to this challenge will build the conceptual knowledge and practical expertise that will contribute to the scholarship, credibility, and professionalization of our field. Also embedded in this priority is development of evaluation methods that address the particular challenges of assessing the impact of work carried out in a context that is: 1) a step removed from the learning of students, and 2) characterized as a collegial and reciprocal learning and problem-solving process. What measures of impact can we use? How can we collect these data? How will the design of evaluation studies influence the climate and substance of work we do with our colleagues? Finding answers to these questions is critical to the continuing development of educational development as a field of practice and scholarship.

A second future challenge is to build scholarly communities of discourse to support our work. Scholarly communities are characterized by shared goals and values; processes of critical inquiry, reflection, and analysis; feedback to peers; debates about ideas, methods, and evidence; connections among ideas and people; and the ability to work collectively toward building our knowledge in a domain (Huber, 2004; Swales, 1990).

Within and across our institutions, we need to build communities of practice and scholarship with colleagues who share interests in learning and teaching (Cox, 2004), including the communications infrastructure; resources; and administrative structures that support, disseminate, and reward this work. Across the educational development community, we need to create and/or enhance local, regional, national, and international networks to improve, critically examine, and share effective practice. Developing these scholarly communities will contribute to our collective knowledge about educational development and provide learning opportunities for colleagues who wish to join our community. Our work together on this project has demonstrated to us the practical and intellectual value of participating fully in such a community.

When we undertook this Mobility Project, we did not anticipate that one of the outcomes would be a framework that conceptualizes our shared practice and scholarship in educational development. The conceptual framework and competency map we present in this chapter are open invitations to educational developers and interested colleagues to think with us about how these tools might inform our work. Questions that could frame the process include the following: Do these tools help you clarify educational development missions and mandates and specify your concept of educational development? Do these tools help describe successful strategies, articulate a set of ethical principles that guide daily work, and create a program evaluation plan? We hope you will join us in answering these questions in the private context of your local practice; in the public conceptualizations of our work; and in the shared community of discourse in which our knowledge is understood, built, and elaborated.

References

Amundsen, C., Saroyan, A., & Gryspeerdt, D. (1999, April). *Learning to teach in higher education: A situation of missing models.* Paper presented at the annual meeting of the American Educational Research Association, Montreal, Canada.

Austin, A. E. (2002). Creating a bridge to the future: Preparing new faculty to face changing expectations in a shifting context. *Review of Higher Education, 26,* 119–144.

Becher, T., & Trowler, P. (2001). *Academic tribes and territories: Intellectual inquiry and the cultures of discipline.* Buckingham, UK: The Society for Research into Higher Education & Open University.

Blaisdell, M. L., & Cox, M. D. (2004). Midcareer and senior faculty learning communities: Learning throughout faculty careers. In M. D. Cox & L. Richlin (Eds.), *New directions for teaching and learning: Vol. 97. Building faculty learning communities* (pp. 137–148). San Francisco, CA: Jossey-Bass.

Bologna Declaration. (1999). Retrieved from http://www.bologna-bergen2005.no/ Docs/00-Main_doc/990719BOLOGNA_DECLARATION.PDF.

Brew, A. (1999). Research and teaching: Changing relationships in a changing context. *Studies in Higher Education, 24*(3), 291–301.

Brew, A. (2002). Research and the academic developer: A new agenda. *The International Journal for Academic Development, 7*(2), 112–122.

Brew, A., & Boud, D. (1996). Preparing for new academic roles: An holistic approach to development. *The International Journal for Academic Development, 1*(2), 17–25.

Canadian Council on Learning. (2006). *Canadian post-secondary education: A positive record, an uncertain future.* Retrieved from http://www.ccl-cca.ca/CCL/ Reports/PostSecondaryEducation?Language = EN.

Candy, P. C. (1996). Promoting life-long learning: Academic developers and the university as a learning organization. *The International Journal for Academic Development, 1*(1), 7–18.

Centra, J. A. (1989). Faculty evaluation and faculty development in higher education. In J. C. Smart (Ed.), *Higher education: Handbook of theory and research* (pp. 155–179). New York: Agathon.

Centre for University Teaching (CUT). (2006). *Sondage BSQ 2006. Conseillers et conseillères. Regroupement des centres de pédagogie universitaire* [Poll BSQ 2006. Educational developers: Grouping of the educational development centers]. Ottawa, Canada: University of Ottawa.

Chism, N. V., Lees, N. D., & Evenbeck, S. (1998). Faculty development for teaching. *Liberal Education, 88*(3), 34–41.

Chism, N. V., & Szabo, B. L. (1996). *A study of how faculty development programs document their usage and evaluate their services.* Columbus, OH: The Ohio State University, Office of Faculty and TA Development.

Cook, C. E. (2000). The role of a teaching center in curricular reform. In D. Lieberman & C. M. Wehlburg (Eds.), *To improve the academy* (Vol. 19, pp. 217–231). Bolton, MA: Anker.

Cox, M. D. (2004). Introduction to faculty learning communities. In M. D. Cox & L. Richlin (Eds.), *New directions for teaching and learning: Vol. 97. Building faculty learning communities* (pp. 5–24). San Francisco, CA: Jossey-Bass.

Dall'Alba, G., & Sandberg, J. (2006). Unveiling professional development: A critical review of stage models. *Review of Educational Research, 76*, 383–412.

Diamond, R. M. (1998). *Designing and assessing courses and curricula: A practical guide.* San Francisco, CA: Jossey-Bass.

Diamond, R. M. (2005). The institutional change agency: The expanding role of academic support centers. In S. Chadwick-Blossey & D. R. Robertson (Eds.), *To improve the academy* (Vol. 23, pp. 24–37). Bolton, MA: Anker.

Eimers, M. T. (1999). Working with faculty from different disciplines. *About Campus, 4*(1), 18–24.

Fletcher, J. J., & Patrick, S. K. (1998). Not just workshops anymore: The role of academic development in reframing academic priorities. *The International Journal for Academic Development, 3*(1), 39–46.

Fulton, C., & Licklider, B. L. (1998). Supporting faculty development in an era of change. In M. Kaplan (Ed.), *To improve the academy* (Vol. 17, pp. 51–66). Bolton, MA: Anker.

Gaff, J. G. (2002). The disconnect: Graduate education and faculty realities. A review of recent research. *Liberal Education, 88*(3), 6–13.

Gandolfo, A. (1997). Identifying lurking alligators: An essay on the ethical dimensions of faculty development. *Innovative Higher Education, 22*(2), 135–150.

Gappa, J., & Leslie, D. (1993). *The invisible faculty: Improving the status of part-timers in higher education.* San Francisco, CA: Jossey-Bass.

Glassick, C. E., Huber, M. T., & Maeroff, G. I. (1997). *Scholarship assessed: Evaluation of the professoriate.* San Francisco, CA: Jossey-Bass.

Hart, G. (1997). Modelling a learning environment: Towards a learning organization. *The International Journal for Academic Development, 2*(2), 50–55.

Hativa, N., & Marincovich, M. (1995). Editors' notes. In N. Hativa & M. Marincovich (Eds.), *New directions for teaching and learning: Vol. 64. Disciplinary differences in teaching and learning: Implications for practice* (pp. 1–4). San Francisco, CA: Jossey-Bass.

Huber, M. T. (2004). *Balancing acts: The scholarship of teaching and learning in academic careers.* Washington, DC: American Association for Higher Education and the Carnegie Foundation for the Advancement of Teaching.

Huber, M. T., & Hutchings, P. (2005). *The advancement of learning: Building the teaching commons.* Menlo Park, CA: The Carnegie Foundation for the Advancement of Teaching.

Huber, M. T., & Morreale, S. P. (2002). *Disciplinary styles in the scholarship of teaching and learning: Exploring common ground.* Washington, DC: American Association for Higher Education.

Hutchings, P., & Shulman, L. S. (1999). The scholarship of teaching: New elaborations, new developments. *Change, 31*(5), 10–15.

Karpiak, I. E. (1997). University professors at mid-life: Being part of . . . but feeling apart. In D. DeZure & M. Kaplan (Eds.), *To improve the academy* (Vol. 16, pp. 21–40). Stillwater, OK: New Forums.

Kember, D. (1997). A reconceptualization of research into university academics' conceptions of teaching. *Learning and Instruction, 7*, 255–275.

Knight, P. T., & Wilcox, S. (1998). Effectiveness and ethics in educational development: Changing contexts, changing notions. *The International Journal for Academic Development, 3*, 97–106.

Kouzes, J. M., & Posner, B. Z. (1995). *The leadership challenge.* San Francisco, CA: Jossey-Bass.

Kreber, C. (2002). Teaching excellence, teaching expertise and the scholarship of teaching. *Innovative Higher Education, 26*(1), 5–22.

LaCelle-Peterson, M. W., & Finkelstein, M. J. (1993). Institutions matter: Campus teaching environments' impact on senior faculty. In M. J. Finkelstein & M. W. LaCelle-Peterson (Eds.), *New directions for teaching and learning: Vol. 55. Developing senior faculty as teachers* (pp. 21–32). San Francisco, CA: Jossey-Bass.

Land, R. (2004). *Educational development.* Buckingham, UK: The Society for Research into Higher Education and Open University.

Leithwood, K. A. (1992). The move toward transformational leadership. *Educational Leadership, 49*, 8–12.

Levinson-Rose, J., & Menges, R. J. (1981). Improving college teaching: A critical review of research. *Review of Educational Research, 51*, 403–434.

Lieberman, D. (2005). Beyond faculty development: How centers for teaching and learning can be laboratories for learning. In A. Kezar (Ed.), *New directions for higher education: Vol. 131. Organizational learning in higher education* (pp. 87–98). San Francisco, CA: Jossey-Bass.

Light, G., Drane, M., & Calkins, S. (2005, April). *Assessing the impact of faculty development programs on faculty approaches to teaching.* Paper presented at the annual meeting of the American Educational Research Association, Montreal, Canada.

Lyons, R. E. (2004). *Success strategies for adjunct faculty.* Boston, MA: Pearson.

MacDonald, R. (2002). Academic development: Research, evaluation and changing practice in higher education. In R. MacDonald & J. Wisdom (Eds.), *Academic and educational development: Research, evaluation and changing practice in higher education* (pp. 3–13). London: Falmer.

Marincovich, M., Prostko, J., & Stout, F. (Eds.). (1998). *The professional development of graduate teaching assistants.* Bolton, MA: Anker.

Mathis, B. C. (1979). Faculty development. In S. C. Erickson & J. A. Cook (Eds.), *Support for teaching at major universities.* Ann Arbor, MI: Center for Research on Learning and Teaching, University of Michigan.

Middendorf, J., & Pace, D. (2004). Decoding the disciplines: A model for helping students learn disciplinary ways of thinking. In D. Pace & J. Middendorf (Eds.),

New directions for teaching and learning: Vol. 98. Decoding the disciplines: Helping students learn disciplinary ways of thinking (pp. 1–12). San Francisco, CA: Jossey-Bass.

Neuman, R., Parry, S., & Becher, T. (2002). Teaching and learning in their disciplinary contexts: A conceptual analysis. *Studies in Higher Education, 27,* 404–417.

Palmer, P. (1998). *The courage to teach.* San Francisco, CA: Jossey-Bass.

Professional and Organizational Network in Higher Education (POD). (2002a). *Ethical guidelines for educational developers.* Retrieved from http://www.pod network.org/development/ethicalguidelines.htm.

Professional and Organizational Network in Higher Education (POD). (2002b). *What is faculty development?* Retrieved from http://www.podnetwork.org/development.htm.

Ramsden, P. (1998). *Learning to lead in higher education.* London: Routledge.

Rice, R. E. (1996). *Making a place for the new American scholar.* Washington, DC: American Association for Higher Education.

Romano, J. L., Hoesing, R., O'Donovan, K., & Weinsheimer, J. (2004). Faculty at mid-career: A program to enhance teaching and learning. *Innovative Higher Education, 29,* 21–48.

Rowland, S. (1999). The role of theory in a pedagogical model for lecturers in higher education. *Studies in Higher Education, 24,* 303–314.

Saroyan, A., & Amundsen, C. (2004). *Rethinking teaching in higher education.* Sterling, VA: Stylus.

Schönwetter, D. J., & Taylor, K. L. (2003). Preparing future professors for their teaching roles: Success strategies from a Canadian program. *Journal of Teaching Assistant Development, 9,* 101–110.

Scott, D. C., & Weeks, P. A. (1996). Collaborative staff development. *Innovative Higher Education, 21,* 101–111.

Sell, G. R., & Chism, N. V. (1991). Finding the right match: Staffing faculty development centers. In K. J. Zahorski (Ed.), *To improve the academy* (Vol. 10, pp. 19–29). Bolton, MA: Anker.

Senge, P. M. (1990). *The fifth discipline: The art and practice of the learning organization.* New York: Doubleday.

Senge, P. M. (1999). *The dance of change: The challenges of sustaining momentum in learning organizations.* New York: Currency/Doubleday.

Shulman, L. S. (1987). Knowledge and teaching: Foundations of the new reform. *Harvard Educational Review, 36,* 1–22.

Shulman, L. S. (2002). Making differences: A table of learning. *Change, 34*(6), 36–44.

Sorcinelli, M. D., Austin, A. E., Eddy, P. L., & Beach, A. L. (2006). *Creating the future of faculty development: Learning from the past, understanding the present.* Bolton, MA: Anker.

Staff and Educational Development Network (SEDA). (2005). *Professional development framework*. Retrieved from www.seda.ac.uk/pdf/index.htm

Stark, J. S., & Lattuca, J. R. (1997). *Shaping the college curriculum: Academic plans in action*. Boston, MA: Allyn & Bacon.

Steinert, Y. (2000). Faculty development in the new millennium: Key challenges and future directions. *Medical Teacher, 22*, 44–50.

Stevenson, C. B., Duran, R. L., Barrett, K. A., & Colarulli, G. C. (2005). Fostering faculty collaboration in learning communities. *Innovative Higher Education, 30*, 23–36.

Swales, J. M. (1990). *Genre analysis: English in academic and research settings*. Cambridge: Cambridge University.

Taylor, K. L. (2005). Academic development as institutional leadership: An interplay of person, role, strategy and institution. *The International Journal for Academic Development, 10*(1), 31–46.

Taylor, K. L., & Schönwetter, D. J. (2002). Academic development as institutional leadership: A framework for meeting new challenges. *Research and Development in Higher Education, 25*, 647–654.

Tiberius, R. G., Smith, R. A., & Waisman, Z. (1998). Implications of the nature of "expertise" for teaching and faculty development. In M. Kaplan (Ed.), *To improve the academy* (Vol. 17, pp. 123–138). Stillwater, OK: New Forums.

Wareing, S. (2004). It ain't what you say, it's the way you say it: An analysis of the language of educational development. *Educational Developments, 5*(2), 9–11.

Webb, G. (1996). Theories of staff development: Development and understanding. *The International Journal for Academic Development, 1*(1), 63–69.

Weimer, M., & Lenze, L. F. (1991). Instructional interventions: A review of the literature on efforts to improve instruction. In R. P. Perry & J. C. Smart (Eds.), *Effective teaching in higher education: Research and practice* (pp. 205–240). New York: Agathon.

Wilcox, S. (1997). *Educational development in higher education*. Unpublished doctoral thesis, Ontario Institute for Studies in Education, University of Toronto, Canada.

Wildman, T. M., Hable, M. P., Preston, M. M., & Magliaro, S. G. (2000). Faculty study groups: Solving "good problems" through study, reflection and collaboration. *Innovative Higher Education, 24*, 247–263.

Wright, W. A. (Ed.). (1995). *Teaching improvement practices: Successful strategies for higher education*. Bolton, MA: Anker.

8

VALIDATION OF A CONCEPTUAL FRAMEWORK

The Meaning and Scope of Educational Development

Denis Bédard, Mieke Clement, and K. Lynn Taylor

There is compelling evidence that the once general perception that university teaching does not require any particular expertise beyond knowledge of one's discipline (Rowland, 1999) is finally experiencing serious erosion. The proliferation of postsecondary teaching credentials for faculty (and new colleagues, in particular) in the UK and Australia is one indicator. In North America, there are graduate courses and more comprehensive programs to prepare graduate students for future teaching roles. Although targeted at different stages in early academic careers, these trends recognize the importance and value of a systematic approach to developing teaching expertise among academic staff. Such programs also mark a shift away from university teachers' gaining expertise by trial and error, sometimes followed by reflection on what worked, to a more proactive investment in developing teaching expertise based on research on teaching and learning (Halpern & Hakel, 2003) and on teacher competencies (Arreola, Aleamoni, & Theall, 2003; Staff and Educational Development Network [SEDA], 2005).

Tightly entwined with this trend is the increasing role of educational development expertise in collaborating with faculty colleagues to build teaching capacity. Most Australian, UK, and North American universities, and some European institutions, have established dedicated units to develop pedagogical expertise across individuals, programs, and organizations. Given the fact that most educational development units are less than 40 years old, and that until recently they have been driven largely by the demands of practice, educational development remains an atheoretical activity. In an effort to contribute to the theoretical conceptualization of this field of practice and inquiry, we proposed a conceptual framework in chapter 7. This conceptual tool evolved through the rich exchanges that characterized our efforts to create a practice community of educational developers crossing diverse institutions and national boundaries. We came to appreciate the added value of the framework of common elements that emerged from our discussions for its utility in articulating our shared work. But we also recognized its limitations.

We felt that even though this framework had emerged from experiences in the five national contexts presented in this book, it may not represent the experience of the entire field of practice. The quality of such a conceptual tool, in our view, would depend not only on its capacity to depict theoretically the underlying principles of diverse educational development practices, but also its ability to reflect the specific activities and tasks that practitioners engage in daily. We hypothesized that a good test of the framework's conceptual robustness would be to see whether educational developers recognized their expertise and their practice in this representation. Additionally, its quality would also depend on the extent to which the conceptual representation accommodates the unique institutional realities in which developers perform their duties.

Taking into account these considerations, we felt that it was important to put this framework to the test by asking colleagues to contribute to its validation and elaboration as a conceptual tool. Consequently, we developed a workshop methodology and conducted workshops at three conferences in Europe, Canada, and the United States in 2006–2007 where we discussed the framework with educational development colleagues. In this chapter, we present the methodology and results of the validation of the conceptual framework conducted during these workshops.

Methodology: The Validation Process

Our methodology allowed us to explore the goodness of fit of the framework with practitioners' perceptions of their practice and of the field by inviting educational developers to critically examine our practice-based framework. In methodological terms, this exercise was a communicative validation

(Kvale, 1994) of a framework that opened the conceptual framework to the critical scrutiny of the broader community of practice by engaging fellow practitioners in dialogue. We gained insights directly, from the contribution of the workshop participants, and indirectly, through our own interactions with the three groups. We specifically asked those engaged in the validation process to reflect on the meaning and scope of the practice and scholarship of educational development practice by exploring the following elements of the framework:

- the educational development mission: enhancing the intellectual, physical, and administrative environments that influence teaching and learning capacity in academic communities, and advocating for high-quality teaching and learning;
- the definition of faculty development as educational development;
- the principles, values, and ethics underlying educational development practice: collegiality and respect, evidence-based practice, working in the local context, and a focus on faculty and student learning;
- educational development units: their positioning in the institution, development strategies, target audiences, and the roles of faculty developers;
- educational development expertise: understanding teaching, learning, and academic culture and how to facilitate change; and
- measuring and evaluating the impact of educational development on teaching and learning.

We planned discussions of these topics to take place around two main tasks in each workshop. First, we presented a brief outline of our Mobility Project as background information to help participants understand the origin and goals of the initiative. Second, we presented the conceptual framework in its "original" version (Figure 8.1) and invited participants to assess how the elements of the conceptual framework resonated with their own practice. This first task, planned for 30 minutes, took place in two steps. In the first step, we asked participants, based on their own educational development expertise, to contribute to the framework building process by adding elements that appeared to be missing from the conceptual map, or deleting or rearranging elements judged to be inappropriate or misplaced. They recorded their reactions individually on a paper copy of the conceptual map,

FIGURE 8.1

The Original Emerging Conceptual Framework of Educational Development

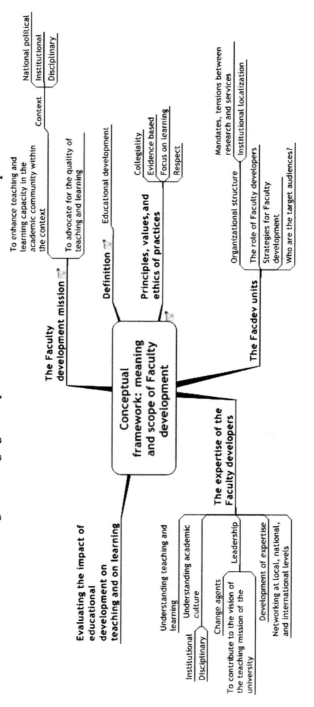

and then shared their versions of the map in small groups of four to five people. In the second step, participants worked in small groups to reach a consensus on which generally applicable elements and relations the map ought to represent.

The second task engaged participants in assessing the framework in light of challenges they experienced in their own institutional context. Still organized in four- to five-person groups, participants were asked to identify three important issues related to their work as educational developers. The group then chose one shared issue and spent about 15 minutes linking it to elements of the conceptual map that helped them to analyze or understand the issue selected. Next, we asked participants to spend about 20 minutes identifying elements in the map that could contribute to solutions or actions to respond to this issue. This step assessed the potential utility of the framework in interpreting issues and formulating responses. Finally, participants were asked to present and share the results of their discussions with the larger group. The workshop leaders ended the session by reviewing the main points presented and obtaining the consent of participants to collect and use copies of their revised conceptual frameworks as data.

Participants and Data Sources

Three groups of colleagues with shared interests in educational development contributed to the validation and elaboration of the conceptual framework. The first workshop took place in Leuven, Belgium, in October 2006 during the first European Conference on Practice-Based and Practitioner Research on Learning and Instruction. Twenty-one colleagues from Belgium, Germany, the Netherlands, the UK, Greece, and Spain participated in this workshop, which we conducted in English.

Participants at this meeting generated nine concept maps on which they had written comments. None of the elements of the original map was deemed irrelevant. Most participants added some explanation to the concepts or suggested synonyms with wider appeal. In some cases, participants added new ideas. It is interesting to note that the notion of expertise provoked the most reaction among the group, suggesting that this dimension requires further research. Overall, the results showed a good fit between the participants' representations and the elements of our original map.

The second workshop took place during the 24th congress of the *Association internationale de pédagogie universitaire* (AIPU—International Association of University Pedagogy) in Montreal, Canada, in May 2007. Thirty-five colleagues participated, including a majority from Canada, complemented by participants from Belgium, France, England, Switzerland, and the United States. As in Leuven, we invited participants to examine the practice-based framework based on their own perspectives. Because French was the language used for this workshop, the material used in Leuven was translated from English to French. Translation introduced some difficulties with respect to finding the appropriate terminology for the concepts in the original map. Sometimes a concept does not translate directly from English into French, even though it refers to the same reality (for example, faculty/educational development versus *développement pédagogique*). In other cases, there were no easy matches for English phrases (for example, to "advocate for" quality).

Although some participants appeared at first to have some difficulty linking the conceptual framework to their practice, engagement in the workshop was very active. We received 23 concept maps on which participants had written comments. A few were suggestions for repositioning elements, and other comments questioned the value or meaning of some elements or added new elements to the existing map.

The third workshop took place during the 32nd Annual Conference of the Professional and Organizational Development Network (POD) in Pittsburgh, Pennsylvania (the United States), in October 2007. This workshop was conducted in English. Eighteen participants, mostly educational developers working in centralized units, actively discussed the conceptual framework. Participants represented diverse higher-education institutions, mainly universities, from the United States and Canada. As in the previous workshops in Belgium and Canada, none of the participants deleted any elements of the conceptual map; they did, however, add a number of comments and suggestions. During the oral presentation of key elements of the map, participants asked questions about specific elements: institutional context (Where do we put institutional mission? Student cultures?); teaching and learning capacity (Should it be interpreted in a broader scholarship of teaching and learning context?); ethics (What does "articulating clear goals" mean? Which goals: the ones of the faculty members? Of the faculty developers?); and expertise (Where are the interpersonal skills and dispositions that faculty developers use in the helping process? Under what conditions do we play a counseling role in helping others?).

Results

The results section synthesizes the discussions that took place in all three meetings. First, it presents participants' suggestions for enhancing the framework, organized along the original six primary components: defining the scope and meaning of the field; educational development mission; principles, values, and ethics of practice; educational development units; expertise required for educational development practice; and evaluating the impact of educational development on teaching and learning. Second, it analyzes the applications participants generated in response to specific practice challenges. On the basis of a matrix of the issues the different groups discussed, we argue that the framework accomplishes, at least in part, the three goals we set for it:

- to articulate an inclusive framework for conceptualizing and analyzing practice across diverse institutional contexts;
- to support the evolution of educational development as a field of practice and scholarship by guiding the initial and continuing education of educational developers and by framing research in the field; and
- to provide a valid framework to frame the evaluation of programs intended to develop learning and teaching (chapter 7).

Conceptualizing the Field

In this section, we describe the results of participants' work on refining the main components of the conceptual framework and the three-stage evolution of the framework to date: the original version (Figure 8.1), the version presented in chapter 7, and the modified version resulting from the three workshops (Figure 8.2).

Educational Development Mission

The original conceptual framework (Figure 8.1) identifies a dual overarching mission for educational development: developing strategies and plans that

FIGURE 8.2

The Meaning and Scope of Educational Development Revisited After the Validation Process

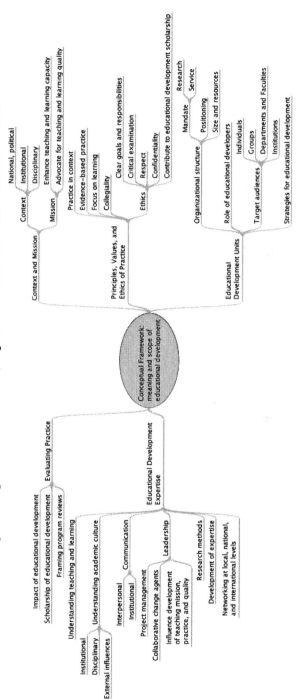

will contribute significantly to enhanced teaching and learning in a particular context, and advocating at a strategic level for quality teaching and learning experiences. This statement regarding the primary educational development mission places a strong emphasis on concrete actions. However, the purpose of educational development is not only to take concrete actions, but it is also to advocate for the quality of teaching and learning through policymaking and strategic implementation of policies. Both dimensions of the mission require developers to understand and be able to work within specific national, institutional, and disciplinary contexts, each of which has its own values, histories, and priorities.

The participants in our three workshops discussed the following common elements of the educational development mission: to create a community of teaching practice within the university; to improve teaching by supporting innovation and updating teaching methods and learning strategies; to respond to the specific expressed needs of faculty; to promote the importance of pedagogy in universities; to facilitate the integration of new professors into their teaching roles; and to reestablish the link between teaching practice and research. They also suggested including making sure that professors receive information disseminated nationally and/or institutionally in meaningful ways—as opposed to formats they often perceived as imposed (for example, ministerial pressures or directives at the national level).

As in our original mapping deliberations, analysis of these data focused not on integrating every aspect of educational development practice identified, but on representing the relationships among those dimensions of practice that crossed practice contexts at a meta-level. With respect to mission, various participant groups suggested that most of the elements of mission fit within the larger themes already identified as nodes in the map, and were judged to illustrate examples of these more general themes. However, one of the changes that became clear to the group conducting the workshop quite early was the strong relationship between context and practice and, in particular, the degree to which context determines mission. Therefore, we adjusted the map before the third workshop to represent context and mission as a combined primary element instead of context as a subelement of mission (Figure 7.1, chapter 7). Educational developers in the third workshop felt this change reflected their experience of practice.

Defining Educational Development

There is abundant literature defining different aspects of the development of teaching and learning capacity, but there is no universal term or single definition for the concept itself. The meaning and scope of development in the domain of teaching and learning appears to be a negotiated phenomenon within each institution (chapter 7). During the course of the Mobility Project, we replaced our original use of the term *faculty development* with the term *educational development*. This perspective focuses on the development of learning and teaching capacity as an *educational development* process: "all the work that is done systematically to help faculty members to do their best to foster student learning" (Knight & Wilcox, 1998, p. 98). Used in this sense, the term was broader than *faculty development*, because it encompassed instructional, curriculum, organizational, and some aspects of faculty development. In another sense, the term was narrower in that it focused on the teaching domain, as opposed to all aspects of academic career development. Notwithstanding this rationale, using these terms in French resulted in some difficulty at the AIPU workshop in Montreal. Subtle differences that sometimes exist between words, in this case, faculty and educational development, cannot be captured easily by equivalent words in French. Non-native English speakers at the meeting in Leuven, Belgium, also mentioned that they had encountered the same difficulty.

The participants in all workshops struggled with the definition proposed, at least as it was explained and presented in this context. Most of the returned maps contained added elements to the definition. It was often suggested that we add the term *coaching* or an equivalent word to the definition. Some recommended including technology in the definition to capture the range of their own practice. Others wrote about the multitasking nature of what they do and felt that ought to be reflected in the definition. Overall, there were as many question marks on the copies as there were suggestions. Ultimately, we decided to eliminate the definition node from the framework (chapter 7). Instead, we recognized that the meaning and scope of *educational development* in any given context is a function of the synergy among the other five primary dimensions of the framework, and therein lies the more detailed definition.

Principles, Values, and Ethics of Practice

Most educational developers are guided in their practice by the principles underpinning their work. The map suggests that, across practice contexts, common principles provide the foundation for educational development models: working in the local context, evidence-based knowledge, a focus on learning, and collegiality. Reflected in these principles are the values and ethics that underlie the practice and scholarship of educational development.

Selected elements of this primary component resonated very positively with most workshop participants, and they engaged actively in elaborating the meaning and application of these elements and their connections to other primary dimensions of the framework. For example, participants perceived evidence-based practice as a positive influence in making links between the development of expertise and the evaluation of the impact of work, which in turn can contribute to the advancement of knowledge in the field. A few participants recommended *nuancing* the meaning of some elements. For collegiality, the word "partnership" was recommended; to respect, the word "mutual" was added; for evidence-based, the words "practice-driven research" were suggested; to focus on learning, the complementary "focus on programs and teaching" was proposed.

Other participants suggested new principles such as the independence that educational developers should have in their relationships with the institution's administration to gain the trust of professors. A principle we added in this regard was *acting with no hidden agenda* (being transparent). Along the same lines, addition of "accountability" was suggested. Yet another suggested element was the need to value communication with professors as well as with educational development colleagues. One participant wrote that educational developers should be responsive to the needs of professors, and that guaranteed confidentiality be an inseparable element of their service to the professors. Finally, one participant suggested adding "continuous professional development of educational developers and faculty" to the list .of principles.

Copies of the maps turned in by participants highlighted some challenges with respect to ethics. The diversity and necessary reconciliation among different cultures on campus was underscored as potentially limiting the ability of educational developers to live the principles, values, and ethics of their beliefs. Another problem was related to educational developers' tendency to propose ideas or innovations without any attempt to assess their consequences on, among other things, learning and perceptions of teaching effectiveness by students and teachers. A third identified challenge was achieving a balance among the activities initiated by the institution, by the educational development units themselves, and in response to requests from professors or academic units. An underlying ethical challenge emerged when colleagues questioned the extent to which educational developers should play a normative role when working in a culture that has traditionally valued individual autonomy. Some workshop participants were comfortable with their roles as institutional change agents (as long as the changes advocated were evidence-based and applied appropriately), whereas others wrote that the educational developers should essentially "pass on" information to the professors instead of trying to push or promote any specific agendas.

These responses reflect the strong impact of local context on educational development practice and the negotiated nature of the role in each institution. We propose that in such a contextually determined role, it is the values and ethics of practice that keep educational developers philosophically and professionally grounded. Consequently, our interpretation and integration of suggestions from colleagues focuses on maintaining fundamental values that allow for diverse expressions across different institutional contexts. One result is that the suggestions for more nuanced articulation were seen to be accommodated within the original values of collegiality, respect, evidence-based, a focus on learning, and the synergy among them in practice. Similarly, a commitment to confidentiality was seen as reflecting the values of respect and collegiality, and a fundamental responsibility to continuing professional development was interpreted as a commitment to evidence-based practice.

The strong concerns some workshop participants voiced regarding the tensions experienced in the roles of educational developers with respect to individual faculty members and to their institutions suggested the addition of another node in the ethics and values domain. In keeping with the strategy of articulating fundamental principles that have the power to ground practice across diverse contexts, we propose the inclusion of articulating *clear roles and responsibilities to all partners* as a principle of educational development practice.

Educational Development Units

Within the contexts in which they serve, the specific roles and organizational structures of educational development units can take diverse forms. Educational development centers most commonly are centralized units directly attached to a senior administrative position (for example, rector/president, provost, or academic vice president). However, increasingly, dedicated educational development resources are being distributed to specific discipline areas such as medicine and engineering. In the experience of our contributing audience, the positioning of an educational development unit in the organizational structure of the institution usually defined the educational development function as well as the strategies for educational development.

Educational development units with closer working relationships with a senior administrator tended to have a stronger institutional-change mandate, even when this mandate was integrated with providing support to individuals with respect to developing their teaching. As a result, participants in the three workshops identified two major (and sometimes concurrent) roles for educational development units: 1) to inform and help professors, and 2) to advise authorities at the institutional level.

The question of who are the target audiences for educational development arises from these sometimes dual roles. The primary target audience workshop participants identified was professors and, particularly, newly hired colleagues. Doctoral and graduate students also make up a significant clientele. It was also suggested that the "indirect audience" (that is, students and faculty not participating in educational development) and "external constituencies and stakeholders" (for example, accreditation agencies) should be considered. Whether the audience is professors, graduate students, or senior administrators, workshop participants linked back to the component of values and principles when they emphasized the paramount importance of collaboration to the success of any enterprise.

Among the challenges this primary component of the framework raised in our discussions was competition among units in the organizational structure of the university, mostly around the issue of financing. The strength of this response warranted the addition of "size and resources" to the educational development unit domain of the framework. Related to size and resources was the challenge of lack of time to accomplish the many activities expected from educational developers. This also places limits on the extent to which we can consider new or innovative opportunities to work. At the same time, participants reported a growing expectation that educational developers demonstrate the impact of their work. This aspect necessarily extends the educational development role to engaging in research and has implications for the knowledge and skill sets required for competent practice.

Expertise of Educational Developers

Few formal programs prepare individuals for careers in educational development. Most people active in the field developed their interests from their diverse careers in and out of academia (McDonald & Stockley, 2008). In a domain where many practitioners learn from experience, the rapid expansion of the practice community means that many educational developers have little experience on which to draw. It is crucial, therefore, to identify the knowledge and skills that educational developers need for competent practice in the field. Workshop participants agreed that educational developers should understand the processes of learning and teaching and the broader activities associated with postsecondary curriculum development and assessment. A small number of participants went further in asserting that it is not enough to "understand teaching and learning," and that it is also essential to demonstrate the ability to "do teaching and learning, keeping a hand in teaching and learning." Much more pervasive among participants were beliefs about the importance of understanding how to apply general principles of learning to diverse disciplinary cultures.

Participants also felt that educational developers should possess the necessary leadership skills to act as "agents of change" and "agents of innovation," especially as such roles pertain to learning and teaching strategies in the classroom (including a balanced use of information technology) as well as with respect to how learning is assessed. Leadership in an educational development context included the ability to advocate for the interests of teaching to both administrators and faculty colleagues. From the perspective of workshop participants, this kind of leadership expertise implied that educational developers should be aware of political and managerial issues in higher education at the national and institutional level. Early in the consultation process, workshop participants also identified the importance of project management skills to effective educational development leadership, and we added this concept to the expertise node in the version of the framework presented in chapter 7.

An area of expertise that we took for granted in the original map, but had to make explicit in discussions with workshop participants, was the ability to communicate effectively across diverse disciplinary cultures and in a collegial way with audiences whose expertise was in disciplines other than the learning sciences. In addition to effective dissemination and translation of knowledge, educational development entails the ability to coach and sometimes counsel others, and participants identified these specific communications skills in the third workshop, in particular. It is this complex skill set that is represented in the communications node.

Another node added in the expertise domain based on workshop consultations was the ability to integrate, design, and do research as well as to present at conferences. Directors of units, in particular, saw operational and management skills (including goal setting, prioritization, timelines, and budgeting) as essential.

Evaluating the Impact of Educational Development on Teaching and Learning

The assumption that educational development has a significant impact on building learning and teaching capacity is the basis of educational development programs. One of the most important challenges centers face is providing evidence that there is a relationship between their activities and improvements or changes in conceptions and practice of teaching. Educational developers need to be able to collect and interpret evidence relevant to activities and outcomes to generate a public account of their work that can be reviewed according to academic standards.

Although many workshop participants identified research skills as an essential area of expertise for educational developers, not all participants agreed that the impact of what educational developers do could actually be measured. They wondered what measures would be meaningful and what evaluative tools and methods could be used. Some suggested that, rather than statistically measuring effects on students' learning, conducting satisfaction surveys that capture dimensions such as "interest toward educational development" and "practical utility of activities" should be the focus. The genesis of these perceived limitations originated in an awareness that educational developers are "one level removed" from the teaching–learning nexus and, therefore, might be claiming undue "credit" for the work of faculty with whom they interact. A similar dilemma exists if we wish to measure the effects of institutional involvement (for example, strategic plans and priorities of senior administrators). Most participants were interested in this dimension of the framework and appreciated its role in the growth of educational development as a field of practice and scholarship. The challenge of how educational developers can accomplish this aspect of their work remains open.

Applying the Conceptual Framework

Workshop participants also applied the framework to challenges they experienced in their work to test whether it had utility in analyzing, interpreting, and solving problems in practice. All three groups reported drawing on elements of the framework in their discussions. One group of participants observed that the map functioned as a "political" tool to present and argue for the value added of faculty development centers, as well as a "diagnostic" tool in solving problems, such as revisiting the organization of one's center. The analysis of participants' responses indicates that the framework does help practitioners to conceptualize issues in ways that facilitate problem solving in their practice.

In reviewing the groups' discussions, it became clear that issues could be differentiated according to the three goals set forth for the framework (Table 8.1).

TABLE 8.1
Overview of Challenges Raised by Participants in Workshops

Designing Practice	Evolution of Practice	Evaluating Impact
Program for teaching and learning in higher education	Implement and develop faculty development centers	Evaluating impact
Fundraising	Set up faculty development center	Measuring impact
Lack of time for innovations (resistance)	Validate activities of existing center	Conducting assessment research and accountability
Responding to multiple actors with opposing demands	Argue for and conduct research	
How to engage teachers in activities offered	Revisit existing organization of center	
Competition among institutions		
Prioritizing		
How to encourage attention to teaching and learning		
Competing agendas for educational developers		
Institutional positioning of units		

In most cases, issues pertained to the design of concrete faculty development initiatives. Participants brought up this 11 times across all three workshops. Quite typically, they discussed challenges they experienced in the design of programs for teaching and learning in higher education. More specifically, they extensively discussed such issues as resistance to innovation and difficulties experienced in engaging teachers in initiatives offered to faculty. In their presentations, participants pointed out that the framework helped to identify crucial elements for success. Respect for teachers and a good knowledge of the particular academic culture were considered important, as were acting as a change agent and advocating for the quality of teaching and learning. When discussing the issue of programs for teaching and learning in higher education, participants realized that they drew on a synergy among values and ethics mentioned in the framework as well as on expertise needed and the mission of educational development.

Other issues regarding educational development practice included competition among institutions, allocation of financial resources, and the fact that educational developers often confront in their work by multiple actors with opposing demands. Again, the framework proved valuable in analyzing these issues further. In their discussions, participants confirmed that it is crucial to have knowledge of organizational cultures and managerial processes as part of their educational development expertise.

As well as issues pertaining to "daily" educational development practice, participants dealt with larger issues related to the evolution of educational development. These activities could be local, as in setting up new centers or revising existing ones, or global, as in conducting research that contributes to advancement of educational development knowledge. Such issues were mentioned five times. In their discussions, participants used the framework to indicate what is needed to develop educational development further as a field of practice and scholarship: a clear mandate, expertise, and an evidence-based approach.

Finally, some groups also discussed the growing need for educational developers to evaluate their work. This issue was explicitly mentioned three times. In all discussions around this theme, it became clear that, according to participants, evaluation of impact is crucial to expanding educational development further and to providing high-quality support in the field. What is not yet clear is how educational developers can achieve this goal.

On the basis of this analysis, consultations carried out in workshops focused strongly on validating those elements of the framework that contribute to understanding faculty development and building effective practice. The choice of issues and subsequent discussions by the groups demonstrate that the framework also has relevance to supporting evolution of educational development at local and global levels, framing research questions about impact, and organizing external evaluations and reviews. Despite these favorable comments that reinforce our work, we recognize that further investigation is needed at these levels.

Conclusion

In our consultations with colleagues, we wished to assess critically whether this framework reflected the activities and tasks in which practitioners are engaging daily. Practitioners who participated in the three workshops in Belgium, Canada, and the United States discussed the elements of the conceptual map. We asked participants to 1) examine the conceptual framework within the context of their practice, and 2) apply the framework to an actual practice issue. Essentially, we wanted to determine the resiliency of the framework in the complex dynamic of cultural and social influences that practitioners experience.

This chapter presents the results of the three workshops. It also attempts to identify the core concepts these three groups consistently recognized as key to educational development across diverse practice contexts. The quality of the discussions that took place showed that, as much as participants appreciated the framework, they also had many suggestions to improve its meaning and content.

We now present the revised conceptual framework developed as a result of our Mobility Project and further consultations with educational development colleagues as an open invitation to educational developers to clarify their mission and mandates; to specify their conceptions and practice of educational development; and to state how their ethics, principles, and values of practice guide their daily work. It also suggests that the ability to articulate educational development expertise and professional knowledge acquired over time is important. Finally, it encourages evaluation of the impact of educational development practice on the intellectual and administrative environment for teaching and learning.

Overall, workshop participants found that the map represented a good fit for their practice and experience of educational development across diverse institutional contexts. It can be considered, therefore, as an effective tool for analyzing educational development knowledge and know-how and for organizing educational development centers and their specific initiatives.

We expected that workshop participants might recognize the potential for the conceptual framework to provide guidance in designing initial and continuing education for faculty developers. However, participants did not mention this potential use of the framework, though one group did work around this issue. In retrospect, this response was not surprising in that workshop facilitators asked participants to focus on the map within the context of practice. Nevertheless, the framework could be considered as a means to design and plan programs for training educational developers, since participants recognized the conceptual framework's utility in facilitating design, implementation, and assessment of educational development initiatives.

We also anticipated that the conceptual framework would provide a context for framing research questions having to do mainly with the impact of educational development. We addressed this component primarily in the application task. However, more than any other aspect of the framework, evaluation of the impact of educational development caused considerable concern among some participants. Some of them raised the question of feasibility in the sense that, since the objective is to improve students' learning by having professors improve their teaching strategies and methods, it would be hard to isolate the educational development effect in an environment that is influenced by multiple factors. In contrast, there was general agreement that such a framework could be used for organizing external evaluations and reviews of educational units and their strategies and activities.

One of the characteristics of the framework that participants mentioned most often was that it depicts well the meaning and scope of educational development. Although the current conceptual map may not be complete, participants recognized that it encompasses the essential elements that should be taken into consideration when one wants to understand educational development practice and scholarship. In light of the results presented, we can say that the goal we pursued to validate elements of the conceptual map was attained for the most part. With the many pertinent suggestions and additions of participants, we expect that the present revised version of the framework will continue to evolve. As Taylor and Rege Colet (chapter 7) suggest, "We invite colleagues to contribute to the elaboration and testing of this framework as a conceptual tool through which we can better understand, implement, and assess learning and teaching development programs."

References

Arreola, R. A., Aleamoni, L. M., & Theall, M. (2003, April). *Beyond scholarship: Recognizing the multiple roles of the professoriate*. Paper presented at the annual meeting of the American Educational Research Association, Chicago, IL.

Halpern, D. F., & Hakel, M. D. (2003). Applying the science of learning. *Change*, *35*(4), 36–41.

Knight, P. T., & Wilcox, S. (1998). Effectiveness and ethics in educational development: Changing contexts, changing notions. *The International Journal for Academic Development*, *3*, 97–106.

Kvale, S. (1994, April). *Validation as communication and action: On the social construction of validity*. Paper presented at the annual meeting of the American Educational Research Association, New Orleans, LA.

McDonald, J., & Stockley, D. (2008). Pathways to the profession of educational development: An international perspective. *The International Journal for Academic Development*, *13*(3), 213–218.

Palmer, P. (1998). *The courage to teach*. San Francisco, CA: Jossey-Bass.

Rowland, S. (1999). The role of theory in a pedagogical model for lecturers in higher education. *Studies in Higher Education*, *24*, 303–314.

Staff and Educational Development Network (SEDA). (2005). *Professional development framework*. Retrieved from www.seda.ac.uk/pdf/index.htm.

EPILOGUE

Kirsten Hofgaard Lycke, University of Oslo, Norway

E ducational development is a rapidly maturing field of practice. In North America and Europe, faculty development programs have taken place since the mid-1960s. International networks for practitioners have run workshops since the early 1980s to expand and exchange ideas based on experiences and theoretical underpinnings. The focus for professional practice over the past three decades has developed from the improvement of teaching to the development of education in a broad sense (Knapper, 2003). As a field of research and systematic development of knowledge, there has been a tendency toward more conscious and scholarly approaches to knowledge building. Boyer (1990), Ramsden (1998), Prosser and Trigwell (1999), Biggs (1999), Land (2001), and others have contributed "a distinctive set of concepts and addressed a core set of issues related to pedagogy within higher education" (Gosling, 2001, p. 87). The first international and scholarly journal for faculty development, the *International Journal for Academic Development*, founded in 1995, has been a motivating force in this respect.

The bulk of these developments, however, has taken place in Australasia, North America, and the United Kingdom. There is still a definite need for scholarly contributions from other countries and cultures, different practices and knowledge bases that can add to our understanding of commonalities and differences in practice and of the concepts and strategies underpinning these practices. To quote Chris Knapper, "One mark of a profession is that practitioners continually explore the conceptual basis for what they do, and debate its emphasis and scope" (2003, p. 5).

Professional developers and others interested in this field undoubtedly will appreciate the contributions of this edited volume. The juxtaposition of case studies of educational development units in different countries and cultures gives insight into and invites reflections on the field as individual readers know it. The conceptual framework contributes to an understanding of the scope and nature of faculty/educational development. In the introduction, the editors and contributing authors of the book set the scene by describing the development of ideas that led to their writing this book. After a thoughtful prologue, five rich case studies are presented: Canada, Switzerland, Denmark, Belgium, and France (chapters 1 to 5).

These studies provide the basis for comparison and reflection on faculty development across Europe and Canada (chapter 6). The book leads to a conceptual framework for educational development grounded in practice (chapter 7) and to a validation of the meaning and scope of this framework (chapter 8). In the following section I look more closely at some of the highlights and perspectives in the book. In the second section, I discuss some of the issues that may be raised in continuation of the materials and analyses presented. In the concluding section, I briefly comment on the possible motivating force for educational change—a wish to contribute to change in higher education.

The Book: Highlights and Reflections

The book presents five case studies based on faculty development and practice in Canada, Switzerland, Denmark, Belgium, and France with emphasis on the period after the Bologna process was initiated in 1999. The case studies are rich in description and perspectives. They constitute a valuable resource, not just for those who are interested in the situation in different countries, but also as examples of commonalities and variations among educational development units regardless of their contextual base.

The case studies show how national differences in the organization of higher education, as well as the political aims, values, and ideologies in this sector, influence and interact with the way faculty development has been implemented. The case studies describe processes and achievements in the sector and invite reflections on how this rather young professional field may be developed further.

The case studies are the basis for a comparison of faculty development across countries in Europe and Canada. The comparison identifies forces that influence the implementation of faculty development in each national context. The major contemporary force in European higher education is the Bologna process. However, the impact of the Bologna process differs among nations, and Hollingsworth and Boyer's (1997) typology categories (markets, hierarchies, states, networks, associations, and communities) are used as analytical tools to understand these differences. The focus is on how these modes of regulation affect developments in higher education and, in turn, faculty development.

The analysis of hierarchies, for instance, indicates that the autonomy of higher-education institutions has been reduced in Belgium and Canada, but has been increased in France in the wake of Bologna. This does not appear to have had a corresponding effect on educational development units; they all have relatively autonomous positions irrespective of national context. Furthermore, when analyzing educational development units of the five case studies according to specific characteristics (Table 6.2), they show noteworthy similarities across countries and institutions. On the descriptive level of the case studies' organizational structure, mandate/mission, and target audience, the units appear very alike. Only the domain of activities appears to vary noticeably in range and content among the units. Belgium and Canada, for instance, have seven almost identical activities, whereas Denmark shares only two of these.

The book next presents and discusses its ultimate objective: to propose a comprehensive model of educational development to view, beyond variations in scope and practices, what are the main dimensions of this field—what is its entirety (chapter 7). A model, or conceptual framework, grounded in practice is detailed, analyzed and discussed, and validated. The authors present this practice through the case studies and in their comparison, and they include the expertise of participants in the project and existing literature on faculty development. The framework maps the field of educational development, and it can help developers and others to identify elements that require attention when designing, implementing, and evaluating educational development activities. The central elements in the framework for educational development are its definition; context and mission; principles, values, and ethics; development units; developers' expertise; and evaluation of impact. The elements are not related to each other linearly or hierarchically, but are presented as organically interdependent and equally important. References to literature underpin the importance of elements.

Development of the framework has raised issues related to terminology. The concepts of *faculty development* and *educational development* have somewhat different connotations in Australia, the UK, and North America as well as among different authors. In general, the term *faculty development* refers to activities that enhance the teaching practice of individual teachers, whereas the term *educational development* refers to more holistic approaches to development at institutional levels. The authors, like others on the subject, argue that the shift from faculty development to educational development signifies not only a change in terminology, but also a shift in the focus of professional practice over the past decades (Baume, 2002; Brew, 2002; Knapper, 2003).

The authors posit that educational development spans "the whole range of approaches . . . : instructional, curriculum, organizational, and professional/academic/faculty development." Furthermore, the authors characterize educational development by "the focus of the range of development activities that are applied and work in synergy to strengthen learning and teaching capacity." Accordingly, the framework includes a broad spectrum of concepts related to educational development.

Another element of the authors' efforts to develop and establish a conceptual framework is a validation process, undertaken methodically in scholarly conferences with contributions from groups of educational developers in Europe, Canada, and the United States. This was done by inviting session participants to undertake two main tasks: 1) match the conceptual elements of the framework with their practice, and 2) apply the framework to a practice issue they might encounter in their work. Different compositions of contributing authors to this volume facilitated the workshops and ensuing activities. Group discussions focused on the central elements of the framework (definition, mission, principles, educational units, developers' expertise, and evaluation of impact). It appears that the conceptual map was a good fit with participants' practices and experiences, encompassing the essential elements of educational development.

The validation of the meaning and scope of the conceptual framework adds an interesting dimension to the book. Readers can follow this process of validation almost as if they were part of it themselves. This underlines the authors' intention not to develop a framework set in stone, but to build a dynamic tool for other educational developers seeking to reflect on their activities with the aim of continuous enhancement.

Issues and New Tracks

This book adds to our knowledge of educational development in a truly international perspective. It invites reflection and alternative perspectives. In addition, the variations and commonalities in approaches and strategies are refreshing and necessary in a relatively new professional field. And so, where do we go from here? In the spirit of the book, it is for each reader, each community of practice, to search for answers. In what follows, I suggest some tracks I think might be worth pursuing: the knowledge base for educational development, the professional educational developer, and international perspectives on educational development.

The Knowledge Base for Educational Development

For an emerging professional field, it is undoubtedly necessary to develop and establish a knowledge base. Such a knowledge base for a professional field should include the theoretical perspectives and the systematized and validated experiences of professionals in the field. On an individual level, it should also include individual professional experiences that are perceived as guiding or critical to practice.

Over the years, broad fields of such knowledge have been developed in relation to educational development. Examples of such contributions include Ray Land's research-based map of orientations of educational developers (2001), Paul Blackmore's categorization of strategies for developers (Blackmore & Blackwell, 2006), and Gunnar Handal's (2007) discussion of the identity of academic developers. But these do not do full justice to the richness and vitality of scholarly work in this field. The *International Journal for Academic Development* (IJAD), national journals, newsletters, and Web sites all demonstrate this point fully.

The framework presented in this book is an attempt to organize experiences and knowledge so we get a clearer understanding of the meaning and scope of educational development. A next step will be to elaborate further the elements of the framework to give it greater substance. What kind of knowledge do we need to fill in the framework? In principle, two types of knowledge are pertinent for educational developers. One we may call *educational* knowledge is related to the knowledge developers use when, for example, they teach or run workshops. This includes knowledge about teaching, learning, evaluation, curriculum, and related aspects of higher education. The other type we may call *developmental* knowledge, which is the knowledge about how to design, implement, and promote educational development. Such knowledge includes knowledge about change and innovation, culture, organization, management, and other insight into the forces and mechanisms that we consider or put into practice as developers.

Both types of knowledge are represented and termed educational and developmental. It may be that the relationship between these two sources of knowledge could be clarified and their relative importance elucidated further. How much knowledge should educational developers have of educational science, including research on teaching, learning, and curriculum? Or is the most important knowledge base to be found in innovation, organizational, and management studies? This clarification process may reveal a need to redefine elements of the framework or restructure relationships among elements.

Such processes may also focus on the meaning of the conceptions. The framework presents six main conceptions, each with a varying number of subthemes. What is the relationship among conceptions in the framework? With a view to using these conceptions as a base for evaluation or research, should we consider them mutually exclusive? Are the conceptions sufficiently clear and understandable? Do they lend themselves well to communication with others? Could the logic behind the presentation be clearer: What elements should be placed above or below, left or right of the axes in the model? Why is scholarship a subset of evaluation instead of expertise? In other words: Do we need to give greater consideration to relationships among elements in an educational development knowledge base? This in no way would reduce the importance of the framework as a contribution to the development of a knowledge base for educational development. On the contrary, the framework is an excellent invitation for further reflection, observation, and testing. The conceptions—even with the annotations in the text—are still open to interpretation. A next step might be to substantiate the conceptions further. If we are to share this as a tool, we need a common vocabulary to communicate with and understand one another.

Another way to flesh out the framework is to compare it in whole or in parts with other conceptual frameworks in the field of educational development. The framework draws on the expertise of the authors and the attempts of others to conceptualize the field. An example is Kreber's (2005) distinction of three dimensions of teaching development: excellence in teaching (skills), teaching expertise (knowledge about teaching), and scholarship of teaching (sharing knowledge that can be peer reviewed). It would be interesting to explore further how such distinctions fit the framework or whether they might contribute to its elaboration. Other examples of frameworks that might lead to interesting comparisons include Land (2001), Ho (2000), and Blackmore and Blackwell (2006). Considering a synthesis based on different frameworks might also prove fruitful.

In stating that the framework is grounded in practice, this book points to a dichotomy that may be easier to state as analytical categories than to identify in practice. Since educational developers have an academic background, we may assume that their experiences are interpreted with reference to, among other things, their knowledge about disciplines and scientific approaches. Theoretical and conceptual understandings influence our experiences and what we regard as important. So it is not a stretch to assert that the understanding of the more theoretical aspects of the educational developers' knowledge base is colored by professional experiences.

Closer inspection often reveals that changes in practice are not based just on experiences with practice, but with new ideas and perspectives on what might be effective—which may or may not be directly related to accumulated experiences. Research on how people learn, for instance, has had a major impact on the focus of workshops, consultations, and other developmental activities. We can use perspectives derived from other types of practice, and we can communicate our own experiences and make them more accessible to other professional fields.

The scholarship of educational developers thus consists of a practice base and theoretical knowledge that are well integrated. Theory helps us perceive and organize the experiences that practice tells us are important. This, in fact, is also demonstrated in the description of the framework where there are a number of references to existing literature to ground included elements.

Some evidence-based practice holds the middle ground between theory and practice. Evidence-based practice is now a buzzword entering our field of practice. Hard facts appear to be valued more highly than are basic principles and accumulated systematic knowledge. Evidence implies that we can identify measurable effect. The concept was originally related to practice in the health sciences and, in particular, medical practice. It is a science paradigm, where the relationship between professional practice and research-based evidence is more transparent and direct than it is in educational practice.

In educational practice, it is more a question of how research and systematic experience can *inform* practice. While we can agree on the importance of evidence of relationships between, for instance, educational development activities and improvements or changes in conceptions and practice, there are problems in producing such evidence. In the existing literature, there are now a number of examples of approaches for research-based evidence of the effects of educational development activities (Ho, 2000; Lycke & Handal, 2004). An example is a well-known study conducted by Gibbs and Coffey (2004) that traces the impact of faculty development activities in eight institutions in the UK and abroad on teacher participants and the learning of their students. They did not find a significant correlating impact on either of these variables.

Even so, the authors of this book are quite right; we do need systematic use of sound research and best-practice literature. We need to be rigorous and systematic in following up the impact of our work, to share our experiences and to be informed by the research of others. One may even argue that this approach is a condition for further development. This book shows one way, and there is a great deal here for practitioners as well as for researchers in the field to learn.

One further point about the knowledge base for educational development should be made. If we are to raise the scholarly status of professional educational development, it will be necessary to show how it relates to other fields—for instance, teaching, learning, evaluation, and management on the one hand, and disciplinary knowledge on the other. We must make these links to bridge the understanding and experience from development work to other disciplinary fields, making educational development less exotic. Even more important, this will encourage raising the standards of our knowledge production and opening the doors to other fields. As it is now, the discourse among scholars in educational development often seems removed from the discourse among scholars studying other educational activities.

The Professional Educational Developer

Another way of further elaborating the framework is by how it may contribute to considerations of the relationship between the knowledge base and what professionals do. What determines what developers do? In principle, our professional actions are guided by our experiential knowledge, the systematized practice-based knowledge of others, and research. In addition, our actions are strongly influenced by our values, ideals, and ideologies.

The previous section focused on the knowledge base for educational developers, but knowledge alone does not determine what professional developers do in practice. The use and application of knowledge is not neutral, but value-laden. We tend to seek out the knowledge that confirms our preconceived views and use it for a purpose we hold to be morally worthwhile.

In other words, educational developers' actions will tend to be influenced by the values in their community of practice and those they prioritize at a personal level. They will be inclined to follow not only what is true or proven, but also what they believe to be good. What kind of university do we strive to have? What do we see as good teaching? What should a teacher be like? Our answers to such questions are related to our values, ideals, and ideologies. Even here we can apply a dual perspective: What kinds of teaching practices are good and right to promote? What kinds of educational development are good and right to strive for? Do our preconceptions direct the way we act?

One perspective on the relationship between conceptions and actions is that conceptions described in a text will have different meanings for different people, and they will elicit different perspectives on the consequences for educational development. The element of understanding learning, for instance, could be taken as implying that there is but one understanding of how learning takes place (Bransford, Brown, & Cocking, 2000). But research on learning over the past decades shows that there are various understandings of how learning takes place. The underlying assumptions about learning processes range from behavioral to constructivist and sociocultural. An important function for the framework may be to help us identify conceptions that have effects on the way we conduct educational development, and to challenge us as developers to delve deeply into how these conceptions affect our practice and our understanding of this practice and how we value these effects.

It is important to bear in mind that the choices we make also depend on the values of educational developers. Do they value the autonomy of the professional or the use of authority and/or collective/individual responsibility? What other values do developers try to promote in their work?

The framework suggests the role and expertise of educational developers as important but separate elements. It might be interesting to try to bring these (and other) elements together in a more holistic understanding of the identity of professional educational developers. Identity is related to expectations, knowledge, actions, experiences, and values. Identity can help bridge our understanding of the expertise and the role with what educational developers, in fact, do. This is not just a question of what types of knowledge the developers have or to which roles they are assigned, but a more fundamental question of what values they strive to realize: What do they see as good teaching? What do they see as well-functioning learning environments?

With the shift in focus from the development of teaching in isolated classrooms to enhancement or change in learning environments, from aiding individual teachers to consultations at different institutional levels, the professional role of the educational developer has also changed and may become more diversified and specialized. In this process, we become not so much experts as collaborators in change processes that might make our professional role less clear-cut than it has been. This may affect our professional ethics. As faculty developers, our loyalty has traditionally been with individual teachers. We have sought to assist teachers in developing teaching that is consistent with our professional knowledge about teaching and learning within a role in which the teachers feel comfortable. As educational developers, our role is now also related to development or change at different organizational levels. It is not necessarily a given that change at one level will be regarded as beneficial or even acceptable at other levels—even if the overall benefit to the institution is indisputable. Will the role of educational developers in this context be clear, or could it be misinterpreted? Will the role be that of midwife or agent of change? Where will the loyalty of educational developers belong: with management or with teachers? What will be the ethical considerations in cases of conflict?

Educational quality exemplifies possible conflicts of loyalty. In recent years, quality as a concept often has become more associated with assurance and control than with development and enhancement. From a management perspective, this may be regarded as an effective and desirable change, but who looks out for traditional teaching and learning values in interactions among teachers and students? If educational developers tilt their attention too much toward organization and system levels, who will be there to support the individual teacher in day-to-day efforts to ensure quality processes?

For many developers, the new role gives them a more strategic place within the organization—and, possibly, higher status. They may become part of decision-making processes of far-reaching importance to the institution and through this work gain unique knowledge of the institution and the sector. This implies new challenges to the professional integrity of the developer: to speak out when necessary to the sector or to society (Knapper, 2003).

International Perspectives on Educational Development

One of the great contributions of this book is its international perspective, bringing together cases of organization and practice of educational development units situated in institutions of higher education within different systems of different countries. The literature in the field has been dominated by North American, British, and Australian traditions and developments in the field. By comparing European and Canadian cases, we get a far more nuanced picture of the field.

The community of practice for educational development has always been highly international to the extent that it is difficult to imagine the status of the field without past and present international collaboration. The early emergence of educational development activities stemmed from awareness of the shortcomings of traditional teaching in higher education. This was not a national phenomenon particular to some countries, but an international trend. In the early stages of the field of educational development, there were few educational developers and units to undertake such work. This created a need for international networking, and participation in such activities has been fairly extensive. This might well explain the common sense of mission and basis/roots for the profession. As an emerging field, it had relatively few practitioners, so international influences through networks, personal contacts, and so-called gray literature were very important. The roots of educational development in a strong but relatively informal international community of practice may help to explain why units in such varied contexts appear so similar.

The book's cross-national comparison of main characteristics of educational units indicates high similarity in mission, organization, and activities. The authors, however, caution the reader and emphasize variations in practices among units: "We need to look between the lines" (chapter 6). The implication is that some differences are not apparent at first glance, or that different practices may take place under the same label.

The influences of international and national forces on higher-education institutions and on educational development are also more complex than might be expected. National forces are filtered through the visions and aims of each different institution within a country; therefore, the institutions can respond somewhat differently to national directives and political signals (Askling, Lycke, & Stave, 2004), resulting in different consequences for educational development. Educational units, however, may also be influenced directly by national policies. Some units have waited to see whether the Bologna process would have an impact on their organization and activities; others have used this process as part of their strategy to enhance their practices or improve their funding.

The apparent commonalities among units in very different national contexts implies a more established field of practice than one might have expected. Educational development units appear to have some fairly stable characteristics that are not easily affected by winds of change from national forces. There is a broad consensus among institutions about the aims and approaches of educational development units and their activities, and educational units themselves seem to have a clear vision of their aims, strategies, and means. It is interesting to note that these characteristics run across both new and more established units; this is quite remarkable in a relatively young profession.

We have seen that this is a commonality arising over time, and it cannot be attributed solely to the Bologna process. However, educational development undoubtedly has taken on new importance through the Bologna process. In many countries, the process has brought about profound restructuring. Educational developers have been confronted with a new set of challenges with very little time to adjust. Through international interaction and collaboration, educational developers now have access to broad fields of knowledge and can exchange experiences.

The tendency for educational development units to be relatively immune to policies affecting other parts of higher education, however, may also give rise to concern. A development practice that is not in tune with the developments of the sector it serves will soon be relegated to a peripheral position. The framework in this book helps us to identify common areas of interest and possibilities for exchanges of resources. As we see, it also contributes to a transparency that increases our awareness of shortcomings and of where educational development itself is in need of innovation.

Conclusion

The rapid changes in higher education have increased the need for educational development competencies. Developers face new expectations and challenges. It becomes more important than ever, therefore, to understand the particular knowledge base for the practice of educational development—perhaps even the limits of educational development as a profession. This book provides a springboard for further scholarly initiatives and developments in educational development. It offers a basis for discussion and inspiration to seek innovation. Furthermore, the book is timely in helping to fill a void, and it should be highly appreciated by both those who "do" educational development and those who make use of such strategies and activities.

References

Askling, B., Lycke, K. H., & Stave, O. (2004). Institutional leadership and leeway: Important aspects of a national system of quality assurance and accreditation. Experiences from a pilot study. *Tertiary Education and Management, 20*(2), 107–120.

Baume, D. (2002). Editorial. *The International Journal for Academic Development, 7*(2), 109–111.

Biggs, J. (1999). *Teaching for quality learning at university*. Buckingham, UK: Society for Research into Higher Education and Open University.

Blackmore, P., & Blackwell, R. (2006). Strategic leadership in academic development. *Studies in Higher Education, 31*(3), 373–387.

Boyer, E. L. (1990). *Scholarship reconsidered: Priorities of the professoriate*. Princeton, NJ: The Carnegie Foundation for the Advancement of Teaching.

Bransford, J. D., Brown, A. L., & Cocking, R. R. (2000). *How people learn: Brain, mind, experience and school. Expanded Edition*. Washington, DC: The National Academies Press.

Brew, A. (2002). Research and the academic developer: A new agenda. *The International Journal for Academic Development, 7*(2), 112–122.

Gibbs, G., & Coffey, M. (2004). The impact of training of university teachers on their teaching skills, their approach to teaching and the approach to learning of their students. *Active Learning in Higher Education, 5*(1), 87–100.

Gosling, D. (2001). Educational units in the UK: What are they doing five years on? *The International Journal for Academic Development, 6*(1), 74–90.

Handal, G. (2007). Identities of academic developers: Critical friends in the academy? In R. Barnett & R. Di Napoli (Eds.), *Changing identities* (pp. 55–68). London: Routledge.

Ho, A. S. P. (2000). A conceptual change approach to staff development: A model for programme design. *The International Journal for Academic Development, 5*(1), 30–41.

Hollingsworth, J. R., & Boyer, R. (1997). *Contemporary capitalism: The embeddedness of institutions.* Cambridge, UK: Cambridge University.

Knapper, C. (2003). Three decades of educational development. *The International Journal for Academic Development, 8*(1/2), 5–9.

Kreber, C. (2005). Reflection on teaching and the scholarship of teaching: Focus on science instructors. *Higher Education, 50,* 323–359.

Land, R. (2001). Agency, context and change in academic development. *The International Journal for Academic Development, 6*(1), 4–20.

Lycke, K. H., & Handal, G. (2004). Faculty development programs in Norway: Status, design and evaluation. In S. Brendel, K. Kaiser, & G. Macke (Eds.), *Hochschuldidaktische Qualifizierung: Strategien und Konzepte im internationalen Vergleich* [Qualifications for university didactics: Strategies and concepts in international comparison] (Vol. 115, pp. 53–70). Bielefeld, Germany: W. Bertelsmann Verlag.

Prosser, M., & Trigwell, K. (1999). *Understanding learning and teaching: The experience in higher education.* Buckingham, UK: Society for Research into Higher Education and Open University.

Ramsden, P. (1998). *Learning to lead in higher education.* London: Routledge.

CONTRIBUTORS

Noël Adangnikou, Université de Bourgogne, France

Denis Bédard, Université de Sherbrooke, Canada

Mieke Clement, Katholieke Universiteit Leuven, Belgium

Mariane Frenay, Université catholique de Louvain, Belgium

James Groccia, Auburn University, United States of America

Anette Kolmos, Aalborg University, Denmark

Kirsten Hofgaard Lycke, University of Oslo, Norway

Jean-Jacques Paul, Université de Bourgogne, France

Nicole Rege Colet, University of Geneva, Switzerland

Alenoush Saroyan, McGill University, Canada

K. Lynn Taylor, Dalhousie University, Canada

INDEX

Also available from Stylus

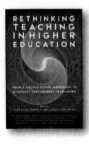

Rethinking Teaching in Higher Education
From a Course Design Workshop to a Faculty Development Framework
Edited by Alenoush Saroyan and Cheryl Amundsen

"The authors provide rich insights into the development of teaching as creative, scholarly work. Their thoughtful analysis is an essential read for everyone with an interest in building teaching and learning capacity in higher education."—**K. Lynn Taylor**, *Director, Centre for Learning and Teaching, Dalhousie University*

Exploring Signature Pedagogies
Approaches to Teaching Disciplinary Habits of Mind
Edited by Regan A. R. Gurung, Nancy L. Chick, and Aeron Haynie
Foreword by Anthony A. Ciccone

"A remarkable achievement that is sure to find its way onto everyone's short shelf of essential books on teaching and learning. The real contribution of the volume lies in the authors' recommendations for how disciplinary fields might develop signature pedagogies that enact and perform the disciplines' core concerns. It also fully demonstrates the claim that teaching, when properly conceived, is exciting intellectual work. Thus, this is the perfect book to give to faculty members who are dubious of 'faddish' education research."—**Lendol Calder**, *associate professor of history at Augustana College, currently represents the Organization of American Historians on the board of the National Council on History Education.*

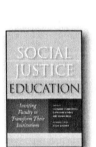

Social Justice Education
Inviting Faculty to Transform Their Institutions
Edited by Kathleen Skubikowski, Catharine Wright, and Roman Graf
Introduction by Julia Alvarez

This book grew out of a project—involving deans and directors of teaching centers and diversity offices from six institutions—to instigate discussions among teachers and administrators about implementing socially just practices in their classrooms, departments, and offices. The purpose was to explore how best to foster such conversations across departments and functions within an institution, as well as between institutions. This book presents the theoretical framework used, and many of the successful projects to which it gave rise.

Learning from Change
Landmarks in Teaching and Learning in Higher Education from Change Magazine 1969-1999
Edited by Deborah DeZure
Foreword by Theodore J. Marchese

". . . provides the reader with a single rich resource from which to draw inspiration, models of good practice, and foundations upon which to build future initiatives. . . The collaborative work contains more than 160 excerpts and articles organized across 13 broadly defined subject areas. Each topic is introduced by experts who help the reader understand the breadth and complexity of the material presented. . . Although the 13 topical chapters are helpful if you are looking for specific categories, I often simply pick up this book and randomly read when I have a few moments to seek inspiration—and I don't think I have ever been disappointed. How many books can make that claim?"—*AAHE Bulletin*

Sty/us

22883 Quicksilver Drive
Sterling, VA 20166-2102

Subscribe to our e-mail alerts: www.Styluspub.com